A Guide to
Successful
Public Relations

A Guide to Successful Public Relations

Colin Haynes

Scott, Foresman and Company
Glenview, Illinois   London

Credit lines can be found on p. vi.

Library of Congress Cataloging-in-Publication Data

Haynes, Colin.
     A guide to successful public relations / Colin Haynes.
         p.   cm.
     Includes index.
     ISBN 0-673-38451-9
     1. Public relations.   2. Publicity.   I. Title.
HM263.H423   1989   88-32261
659.2—dc19   CIP

1 2 3 4 5 6   RRC   93 92 91 90 89 88

ISBN 0-673-38451-9

Scott, Foresman professional books are available for bulk sales at quantity
discounts. For information, please contact Marketing Manager, Professional
Books Group, Scott, Foresman and Company, 1900 East Lake Avenue,
Glenview, IL 60025.

Dedication

To my eldest daughter, Rebecca, who demonstrates one of the basic principles of good public relations—enthusiasm. May the communication business provide her with as much fun and as many challenges as it has her old man.

Acknowledgments

Permission to print public relations stunt using King Kong to advertise Pepsi given by Jack Mayo, President, Mayo and Associates.

Reference to public relations projects of the Delco Remy Division of the General Motors Corporation printed with permission from Keith Pitcher.

Reference to public relations projects of the Chevrolet Motor Division of the General Motors Corporation printed with permission from Ralph Kramer.

Photos on pages 7 and 8 courtesy of Thomas F. McDonald, Director, Central Public Relations, Volkswagen of America.

Quotation of Ron Rogers, President, Rogers and Associates, printed with permission.

Deleo Remy press release, pages 16–41, courtesy of Steven Sterling, Senior Account Executive, Anthony M. Franco, Inc.

Photo on page 62 courtesy of H.D. Calton, Manager, Ford Motor Company, Ltd.

Reference to Parker Pen Company public relations project printed with permission of Eugene G. Rohlman, Manager, Marketing Communications, Parker Pen USA Ltd.

Figures on pages 123 and 126 courtesy of Frank Donadee.

Figures on pages 144 and 188 courtesy of Daimler Benz USA.

Reference to public relations philosophy of Pete Packer, Vice-President, Communications, Runzheimer International printed with permission.

Photos on pages 52, 176, 177, 180, and 181 courtesy of John Perdwyn, Director of Public Information, Goodyear.

Photos on pages 214–216 courtesy of D. Chuck Olsen, Executive Secretary, APRC.

Reference to the Lotus advertising incident printed with permission of Robert Jay Lebow.

Interview with Judith Briles printed with permission.

Reference to "Bread 'n Jam" public relations project printed with permission of Robert Jones, Media Relations Consultant, Lincoln National Corporation.

Interview with Dean L. Fox printed with permission.

Reference to public relations project featuring Adidas footwear printed with the permission of the Director of Public Relations, Adidas USA, Inc.

Reference to the IABC Gold Quill award printed with permission of Norm Leaper, President, International Association of Business Communicators.

Reference to audiovisual presentation by Dr. Mark A. Gillman printed with permission.

Photo of Kashan Tree of Life Prayer rug courtesy of Sotheby's, Sussex.

Reference to the campaign of Art Agnos, Mayor of San Francisco, printed with permission.

Interview with Patricia Guy printed with permission.

Contents

Section 1

Good PR Is Two-Way Communications—Inside and Out
Listen to learn and get focused   2

Section 2

Section 3

Section 4

Section 5

Introduction

The publicity and image-building business has largely failed to project a positive, healthy image of its craft to the media people, who are the targets for so many PR products, and to the business clients who pay—often very handsomely—for services that frequently are not understood properly or used most effectively.

This book sets out to try to correct some of those misconceptions from the viewpoint of one who has been involved with the PR business for over 30 years, from the triple perspectives of journalist, client and PR consultant.

The examples of imaginative, competently executed communication programs demonstrate what a challenging and satisfying occupation PR can be, with the ability to offer tangible benefits to businesses and other organizations as well as to the sectors of society that they serve. They should stimulate other PR professionals in their work and provide an additional insight into the value of a much-abused profession.

The case histories show what a mistake it is to regard the most significant PR as being undertaken only with big budgets, on a national or international level, and with brilliance in conception and execution. We are all influenced in our daily lives by public relations activities carried out on a small scale with limited resources and executed in what might appear to be a routine, mundane fashion. Often these activities are at a local level, in our own community.

The person responsible for day-to-day PR for a local hospital, a small company, or perhaps a voluntary organization has a very important role to play and, I hope, will derive benefit from this book and be able to adapt the examples to his or her own situation. The basic ground rules for such practical activities as preparing media releases and developing trusting relationships with media people apply as much in contracts with your local newspaper as they do to dealing with *The New York Times*.

Good communication always start with quality listening. You will find many examples of how a product was promoted, a message conveyed, or an image improved simply because the PR people involved took the trouble to listen to the needs of their target audiences and those at all levels within their own organizations or employed by their clients who were able to provide valuable input.

Far too often, PR reflects a lack of sensitivity to the needs and feelings of those affected by a particular communication exercise, whether it be consideration for journalists bombarded with media releases useless for their requirements or employees continually alienated by finding out only from the public media about developments in their own company. That reflects a corporate attitude of neither talking nor listening to the people who are its most valuable resource.

The most neglected of PR fields is internal communication. Companies—indeed, most organizations—spend a disproportionate amount of time, effort and money on promoting their goods and services to their external audiences, in most cases, their markets. The customers may experience better communications than do the people who commit their working lives to producing those products and services.

That's all wrong—and is proving to be very bad business. Employees are "demotivated"—to the point of open hostility—if they do not feel trusted with important information and fully recognized as valued participants in any enterprise. Demotivation and hostility can soon turn to open or subconscious sabotage of corporate objectives.

There are horrifying statistics about the negative attitudes of American workers, which should cause a lot of gleeful hand rubbing in Tokyo and Frankfurt, although the Japanese and the Europeans are experiencing similar difficulties to varying degrees.

Surveys indicate that three out of every four American workers feel that their company communicates badly with them. The blame for that situation must be shared—by managers, by unions and often by the workers themselves. You cannot critize the PR practitioner more than anyone else over the failure to communicate to employees, because management has not recognized that internal marketing is as fundamentally good for business as is external promoting to customers.

Effective PR can make a significant contribution to correcting this business malaise. I keep returning to this theme throughout the book because it is so important—perhaps the biggest challenge facing PR professionals. It is not a task best left to the human resources people, because they rarely have adequate training in specialist communications techniques. Employee communications should be a growth area in which PR professionals practice their skills and perhaps make new and very rewarding careers.

Enough preaching. Enjoy the book. I hope you will come to share my respect for the many people whose high professional standards are reflected in it.

Colin Haynes
San Francisco

Section 1

Good PR Is Two-Way Communication— Inside and Out
Listen to learn and get focused

PR is not an exercise in one-way communication. Indeed, the best programs *always* start with a lot of listening. You must go out, ask questions and really listen to the responses in order to get input that will enable you to focus your program by defining clear objectives and the right way to achieve them. This principle surfaced over and over again in the hundreds of case histories I evaluated while writing this book. The best PR people are not necessarily the best speech makers or presenters, but they are the best listeners. The negative image which handicaps the industry is because it has attracted so many of the wrong people, who see in promotion, publicity and communications generally a way of projecting themselves for a whole host of reasons, most of them selfish.

A classic example of the value of listening was seen when the New York Chapter of the Public Relations Society of America gave one of its Big Apple Awards for Excellence to the Burson-Marsteller agency for the Glaxo Pathway Evaluation Program. Let's look at it in detail.

Glaxo was the fastest-growing pharmaceutical company in the United States and obviously needed to forge a long-term relationship with future doctors. This could be achieved by getting closer to medical educators and their students.

The 1987 budget for this task could have been spent in many conventional ways, but the essential first step of research—listening to the needs of the target audience—led to an unconventional solution to a complex problem.

IDENTIFYING NEEDS

The essential premise was identifying the *needs* of the target audience. Those needs were revealed by a series of detailed interviews with the deans of medical schools, association program directors and medical students.

The students expressed a real need for career guidance in choosing a medical specialty during the third year of medical school study. Here was a gap which Glaxo not only could fill but could make its own with a proprietary program that would bond it to many future doctors.

As the program was implemented, Glaxo and its PR consultants continued to listen. They recruited an advisory board of medical school deans to guide the program and to ensure that it remained relevant to the needs of the students.

Implementation was a multimedia activity, with everything well-tested along the way. Three-hour workshops at the participating medical schools set the ball rolling and have become a permanent feature of an ongoing program that is highly valued by those whose interests it serves.

INVALUABLE DATABASE

A workbook was developed to help students assess both themselves and over 30 medical specialties and workshops are being introduced to all 127 medical schools in the United States. The growing database of students who participate in the program will give Glaxo an invaluable continuing means of keeping in touch with the young doctors as their careers develop.

Such a good idea cried out to be publicized more extensively—to a wider audience—as a general image-boosting exercise for the sponsors. A press conference, therefore, was held at the New York Academy of Sciences—it always helps to choose a venue with status and credibility. That activity resulted in over 13 million editorial impressions (published or broadcast exposures) that have further accelerated the program along by stimulating numerous additional enquiries.

None of those PR successes—or the creation of a valuable service to the medical community—would have been achieved without the essential first step of listening to the needs of the target audience.

LISTENING IS AN ART

It horrifies me to sit in presentations in which overconfident or inexperienced PR people announce with great confidence actions that should be taken, before they have had adequate opportunity to listen and so get informed input to guide them in developing a strategy.

Good listening is an art that can be acquired and taught, yet scant attention is given to it in most PR training. It should not be confused with factual research. Much research is too often limited to fact finding and may be a completely negative exercise if it is undertaken in a highly formalized way with rigid preconceptions. You can use research to prove anything, but listening and paying attention to the nuances of the feelings, attitudes, and needs of your target audience comprise an exercise in sensitive two-way communication, which can pay handsomely.

It did so for another Big Apple Award winner for the same agency in which quality listening resulted in the Shelter Aid program sponsored by Johnson & Johnson.

MAKE YOUR CREDO WORK

I have undertaken work for J&J, and it is a delight to be involved with a company that really believes its credo and implements it in positive ways to demonstrate a desire to be a good corporate citizen. That positive corporate image was reinforced by the Shelter Aid program because the company actively explored with the National Coalition Against Domestic Violence how J&J could best apply efforts and resources to most effectively serve the needs of women and their children who face domestic violence. The result was a trial-blazing program that increased awareness of the domestic violence problem and, through a national coupon redemption effort, raised funds to support member shelters of the National Coalition Against Domestic Violence and establish the first national toll-free hotline to give readily accessible help to the many women who are victims in their own homes.

This was a large operation involving a donation of over $1 million, but it was not just "big bucks" that made it work. There has been a ripple effect of volunteer effort, which has produced valuable additional input.

Shelter Aid is a good human interest story and resulted in over 1,000 positive media placements, 90% of which mentioned J&J.

GOOD WORKS SCORE

You really can score with good works, even when they are linked strongly to commercial objectives. Hoechst-Roussel Pharmaceuticals did it with the Leg Alert campaign to encourage early diagnosis of peripheral arterial disease. Pizza Hut made a significant impact on illiteracy with its Book It! national reading incentive program.

Book It! was a massive operation that cost $2.7 million to administrate, involved 7.1 million children in the United States during 1985–86, and resulted in the distribution of $50 million worth of free pizza. It was not a conventional promotion, although it was more cost-effective in promoting products and corporate image and spreading awareness and positive feelings about Pizza Hut than many conventional promotions would have been.

Teachers, students, and parents were all involved in a reading program with specific goals and awards, which attracted an enormous number of people to Pizza Hut outlets. There was quality listening at the beginning to define the needs of the target audience, which were clearly met. The average number of books read by participating students increased threefold, 77.5 percent increased their reading enjoyment, and there was a positive improvement in general attitudes towards learning.

I could fill this book with PR campaigns in which quality listening was the real key to success. It is not a passive exercise to be delegated to researchers but an invaluable function in which all communications personnel involved in any program should participate.

INTERNAL COMMUNICATIONS NEGLECTED

Listening to employees can be particularly valuable, for both generating external-publicity material and achieving effective *internal communication,* that grossly neglected area of PR activity. Indeed, listening to your employees can be far more effective in both time and cost than surveying your customers. Internal communication must be effective in both directions to generate good PR. The answers you seek to a PR task are probably within your organization—if only you ask.

Some companies do the asking on a big scale. AT&T regularly finds out what 120,000 employees are thinking and feeling in a survey that is one of the largest of its kind outside the U.S. Census. Hewlett-Packard has grown into one of our biggest and most successful computer hardware companies by means of its ongoing policy of regular two-way dialogue with its employees.

H-P's David Packard made strategic policy decisions to enable him to continue to use his human resources effectively through internal PR as his company began accelerating from the critical start-up entrepreneurial phase, growing into a large organization with the consequent inevitable complications of size in maintaining good internal communication. When his workforce reached 2,000, Packard sent out warning signals on the vital need to maintain communication among his people. They still benefit from efficient internal communication now that H-P has over 80,000 employees worldwide, and 4,000 people in the United States alone apply every month to join this model of a corporate family.

INTEGRATE QUALITY COMMUNICATION WITH THE CORPORATE CULTURE

Communication at all levels is an integral part of H-P's corporate culture. Managers even use the employee attitude surveys as a way of feeding their ideas to top management and colleagues who may be able to help develop them.

In some companies, such tactics may be the only way a frustrated manager can communicate. That is why the writers-at-large or the PR people in big organizations frequently find savvy managers using them in all kinds of obscure ways. H-P's internal communications flow freely in a plethora of means and directions. One of the most effective is the MBWA concept, "management by wandering around", in which managers go out from their offices and circulate with purpose to become accessible and interface with their colleagues and subordinates. An open office layout physically facilitates such contacts.

PR people would do well to regard "wandering around" word-of-mouth communication as a powerful medium that should be considered in any media mix. There is also an important timing consideration: ensuring that major developments are communicated

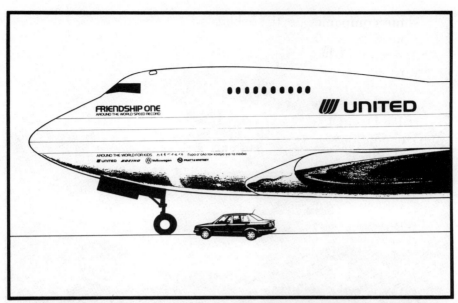

Get the picture to tell the story as much as possible. Volkswagen does it well in this shot of their Jetta in front of the United Airways Boeing 747, which flew it around the world to break records, raise funds for children's charities, and generate PR exposure for the sponsoring companies. This line drawing was created also to give publications an alternative visual that would reproduce easily.

to the workforce in this way—or by more formal means, such as the company newspaper—*before* an external release is issued. Morale can be damaged badly when employees feel that they learn about important developments affecting them and their corporation only or for the first time in the public external media.

PAYOFFS FROM LISTENING AND COMMUNICATING

There are many important payoffs for companies that listen and communicate well internally. For example, when markets decline, as must inevitably happen in any industry, companies like H-P get the strategic benefits of having a workforce motivated to make sacrifices because they are well-informed about how short-term suffering can lead to long-term benefits for themselves and the company. When

The VW stunt—making the car the fastest in the world by being on board the jet-liner when it broke the world circumnavigation record—seems rather contrived, but acquired more validity by raising $500,000 for children's charities. A charity tie-in is a regular PR ploy which gives a rationale and evokes greater media sympathy for even the most bizarre publicity-seeking promotions.

The accompanying Volkswagen press releases are ingenious in plugging the car's features—including the fact that it accelerates to 100 miles per hour 2.5 seconds faster than the Boeing does. The follow-up to the stunt was a good example of generating additional publicity returns, with the car touring U.S. auto and air shows and appearing at important motorsports events.

business sagged in the early seventies, everyone from boardroom to factory floor in H-P took a 10 percent cut in salary and a one-in-ten extra day off. As a result, when trading conditions improved, H-P, unlike many of its competitors, had its skilled workforce in place and was able to build up speed again quickly and economically.

FINDING THE RIGHT DIRECTION

Sometimes even a limited, small-scale consultation with employees can be incorporated with internal PR activities to point a company in the right direction. Avon Cosmetics divested from an unsatisfactory alliance with Tiffany's that could have been horrendously expensive. A sounding of employee attitudes showed that the philosophies and views among employees in the two companies were so different that a merger made no sense at all.

Similarly, American Express found out, when it took a sounding of the attitudes of its executives, why its acquisition of Fireman's Fund was not gelling. Amex succeeds by being an efficient money machine, churning over the cash it collects at a furious rate. Liquor stores and supermarkets do this on a smaller scale by running to the bank several times a day to deposit takings and to get their profits working for them fast, while slowing down their expenditures by seeking extended terms from their suppliers.

The attitude, philosophies and methods of working of Fireman's Fund were so different that the merger of the insurance company with Amex never really stood much chance of working out in the long run. Amex turns its money over fast and is very much a "today" operation, which colors its whole corporate culture. Fireman's Fund, as an insurance company, might not know for 20 years if the deal it strikes today will prove to be profitable. The paper figures and physical resources of Amex and Fireman's looked like a good match, but an investigation of the people and their attitudes showed that a close marriage was unwise.

EXAMINE THE PEOPLE ISSUES

It is the failure to look more closely at people issues in mergers and acquisitions that causes the current high failure rate. Most such corporate marriages end in divorce within seven years. In contrast, when companies come together in a natural blending of their human resources, the success rate is much higher. Almost invariably, good internal PR and a real effort to listen to employees figured prominently in the cultures of the successful companies.

Listening to its employees and motivating them enabled American Airlines to make a number of strategic decisions by which it avoided being the target of a hostile takeover and saved it from being forced into unsatisfactory marriages. AA undertook its famous "Quality of Life" study about the time of deregulation and learned a lot from its employees as well as its customers.

Both the external and internal "customers" of many airlines at that time had even less loyalty to these carriers than they did to the brand of cigarettes they smoked or the TV programs they watched. AA approached these internal and external human issues as part of their strategic planning, and so acquired some very valuable PR cards to play when the chips were down. AA's PR timing was perceptive also, particularly in the way it held back implementation of many of the findings of the Quality of Life study for over a year until exactly the right moment to play this trump card.

MOTIVATE EMPLOYEES

Now many airlines have major internal and external image problems because their relationships with their employees are so poor. They move into an era in which service may outpull fare discounting in the marketplace, with their main interface with their customers—the flight attendants—poorly motivated and badly informed.

When Tiffany's wanted to know more about their target market for $100,000 necklaces, they did not need an expensive customer survey to get their marketing strategy right. They asked their salespeople, who have well tuned antennae and can identify the big buyers the moment they step through the doors from Fifth Avenue—whether they are wearing Guccis or sneakers.

PICK EMPLOYEES' BRAINS

John Hancock's memorable series of TV commercials, which ran during the Superbowl and had the 800 numbers jammed with responses, originated by picking employees' brains. The top management knew it had a wide range of financial services that were underutilized. John Hancock could have commissioned very expensive research to find out why they were not selling, but its field sales force had the answer at the tips of their tongues and—when asked—pointed out the defects in their customers' perception of the company. So John Hancock ran a campaign that zeroed in on those customer misconceptions, and the next quarter was the best in the company's history. In other words, management filled an external-communication gap by using their internal human resources through effective communication *with* their workforce.

TACKLING TRAUMA

Using these resources really works when a company is in trauma—and that trauma can come as much from the stresses of too-rapid growth as it can from the crisis of a hostile takeover or a dramatic fall in sales.

Sensitive PR people, just like the experts in employee attitudes, can spot problems in corporate cultures as quickly as a Tiffany salesperson sniffs out a big buyer. A leading employee attitude researcher told me how, when visiting a potential client, he had hardly passed through the door before he was able to identify the root causes of poor productivity. The computers were housed in carpeted, air-conditioned splendor, the employee restrooms and cafeteria were hot, dirty, and generally disgusting. That symbolized attitude problems on the part of the employers, not the employees.

"Of course you cannot run a company when you treat your machines with more consideration than your people," he said. "So often human resources are just not regarded as assets to nurture and protect. Some managements are even resistant to survey employee attitudes because they not only don't care, they are apprehensive about learning what their employees think of them. That is as foolish as not getting a medical test because you fear the results and so delay treatment until it may be too late."

THE POWER OF RUMORS

Rumors are extremely powerful and can wreak havoc with a PR strategy, especially one for a company with employees who are not motivated to support their company's missions. This is especially so in an era in which the media are so accessible and aggressive, readily responsive to stories fed to them by "inside sources" . Make sure that the workforce will support the organization's external PR efforts by having carefully timed and effective internal PR as a key part of the program.

Annual Reports

A powerful PR communications tool inside and out

Any company that believes preparing an annual report is just a way of keeping the investment community happy is way out of step with the best contemporary PR. In addition, to put undue emphasis on slick design, full-color printing, and lots of statistics just compounds the many lost opportunities in the annual report paperchase, which takes place at vast expense.

A prime target audience for annual reports should always be the workers who have made those impressive bottom-line figures possible. There are valuable lessons to be learned in how the order of priorities was spelled out for the Pillsbury Company's annual report to employees, which so deservedly won an International Association of Business Communicators' Award of Excellence.

At the top of the list was crediting employees for the company's success. Second was communicating how the company's missions and values were being personified through its many businesses and employees. The third priority was that the quality of presentation in the employee report would equal that in the one directed at stockholders, underlining the company's appreciation of the value and importance of both audiences.

The Pillsbury employee report, which won the IABC Gold Quill award in 1986, provides many lessons about the value of a clear, simple approach which always bears the target audience in mind. While it starts with a message from the CEO in the conventional way, this is brief and unpretentious and is complemented by the corporate Mission and Values Statement—a recommitment to the credo.

DON'T BE BORING!

The rest of the publication breaks away from the boring traditional pattern of putting the various business activities into separate sections, resulting in a rigid, uninteresting structure. Instead, Pillsbury used many employee profiles, which are easy to dip into and high in human interest. That format gets across the facts in an entertaining way and fosters the image of a large group in which the employees belong to a single, cohesive corporate family.

This emphasis on Pillsbury's people was graphically underlined in a clever way by superimposing the signatures of those featured over their photographs. The visuals gain impact by using a 10½-inch-wide by 11-inch-deep page and by varnishing to give a glossy, high-quality finish.

COMMUNICATING THE CONSEQUENCES OF A MERGER

Another excellent example of creating a report directed at employees comes from Australia, where the Coles Meyer group used the report format to make 55,000 employees aware of their successes following the merger of the country's first and third largest retailers.

Greg Every masterminded the exercise and, with a budget of only $25,000, still managed to produce an impressive publication printed in four colors throughout on a heavy stock and with a laminated cover. This was no cheapie and, like the previous example, underlined the regard in which management held the workforce.

Greg got the managing directors of each business in the group to submit copy, but then only lightly polished and edited their words so that the personalities of the executives still came through. Photographs reflected a major event that took place in each business group during the course of the year—generating far more interesting visuals than the boring static shots of plant and equipment that predominate in so many annual reports. Another benefit was that the variation in content of the photographs built up an overview of the diversity of the new group as a result of the merger. Other important features were descriptions of employee benefits and a bound-in employee questionnaire to stimulate two-way communication.

Greg showed that a lot can be achieved on a tight budget. The task is made considerably easier if you exploit the advantages of desktop publishing. The following example also illustrates how the annual report can often be combined with other communications objectives into a single publication.

CUTTING COSTS

When Bob Reznik, vice-president of marketing at the Texas Back Institute, wanted a high-quality combination annual report and journal on back care to increase awareness of the institute among a diversified target audience, he got three design agencies to bid for the project. By designing and typesetting it directly off a Macintosh Computer into a Linotron 300 he stripped $15,000 off their production costs.

Let us delve deeper into the cost-cutting efforts that featured in Bob Reznik's 1987 Gold Quill Award–winning report, because it contains many practical pointers to the ways a shrewd communicator can stretch budgets.

There was a legacy of disputes over billing from the telephone company—and experienced PR practitioners and advertising people know how often that happens! Bill negotiated the telephone company's claims into a $12,000 discount on $50,000-worth of Yellow Pages advertising. He also got $200,000 in concessions as a result of former business ties to another organization and saved $25,000 annually by setting up an in-house agency to purchase advertising space at 15 percent below retail cost.

Those savings from media commissions were used to employ a salesperson to visit physicians and chiropractors and thereby achieve a ten percent increase in the volume of their patient referrals to the institute.

FOCUS ON THE BEST PERFORMERS

It is sometimes difficult to cover a wide range of individual employees in an annual report and better to focus on a few groups who have performed outstandingly and who have particularly interesting stories to relate. Paul F. Pickard combined both techniques in the first annual report to employees by Orange and Rockland Utilities, Inc.

When featuring employees in any report or other medium, try to cover a wide range of levels in the corporate hierarchy and a diversity of activities. Orange and Rockland Utilities featured the extra-high-voltage line crew, perceived to be a glamorous and potentially dangerous activity. The story on an underground-line quality circle showed how its members came up with an ingenious solution to a safety and reliability problem. Another feature focused on the commercial operations team's successful priority service program for builders.

Employee feedback was very positive and there was a clear appreciation of how the "little guys" in the company were being recognized for their contributions.

THE TRAUMA OF CHANGE

I would particularly recommend the employee report when a company is going through some kind of trauma, perhaps as the result of a merger or take-over or the introduction of new technology. One of the most traumatic of technological innovations is the introduction of robotic applications to manufacturing plants. Such technological developments can yield good copy for both external and internal PR use.

These are situations in which training and PR expertise should work hand-in-hand. Internal PR can work wonders in improving the quality and productivity of a workforce and should form part of any program.

Steven Sterling, of the Detroit PR agency Anthony M. Franco, Inc., has produced examples of how the internal changes in a company can make good promotional copy for external audiences in the features he has written about automation at Delco Remy, which produces many of the components and subassemblies in the automobiles we drive.

He has allowed me to critique his special feature for the magazine *Automation* in detail. Here it is, with my comments alongside.

(A)
FOR: GMF ROBOTICS

FROM: ANTHONY M. FRANCO, INC.   CONTACT: Steven Sterling
          400 Renaissance Center   (313)   567-2300
          Suite 600
          Detroit, Michigan 48243

(B)
<u>PRODUCTIVITY AND QUALITY JUMP</u>
<u>AS FLEXIBLE AUTOMATION</u>
<u>COMES ON LINE</u>
<u>AT DELCO REMY</u>

                              SPECIAL TO: AUTOMATION

(C)
"If you do not think about the future you cannot have one."
                    John Galsworthy

(D)
(E)
      Delco Remy is not just thinking about its future.

This division of General Motors is doing something about it

by boosting its competitive edge through flexible

automation.

      At Delco Remy facilities across the country, flexible

systems based on robotics are achieving significant gains

in productivity and quality. Consider the following:

* Flexible automation has slashed final assembly cycle
   time by more than 20 percent.

* Delco Remy has reduced by 200 percent the number of
   finished units that do not meet specifications at the end
   of the assembly process.

* Warranty claims have decreased by 150 percent as compared
   to preceding products.
                              (F)

The source of the story and contact address and telephone number are right at the top, where they should be. You might also include here a word count indicating length. Most word processing programs will do the sums automatically for you.

The headline could be punchier, as the editors at *Automation* have made it with their version: Flexible Automation Ups Quality & Productivity. It was a brave try to put the client name in the heading, but this time we didn't get away with it!

I like the quote. In this case, Steven has used a classic literary quote. An alternative would be to pick a contemporary quote from within the story, which the editor can use as a breaker in the layout.

It was fair to start the story with the company name because the target publication is an industry-specialist magazine, but usually it is better to go for a softer sell and highlight a key newsworthy fact. For example, the release could have begun:

"Flexible automation has slashed final assembly cycle times by over 20 percent, cut rejects by 20 percent, and decreased warranty claims by 150 percent at Delco Remy".

Put "more" or "m/f" (for "more follows") at the bottom of every page except the last, which should clearly state "end".

(G) Page Two

Delco Remy is also demonstrating that productivity and quality gains are not the only benefits to come from flexible automation.

* Because robots can be reused, management estimates savings of up to 66 percent savings on retooling costs as product lines change.

(H) * On machining lines where robots have been installed, material utilization has doubled.

* The time it takes to get a robot up and running on a new job is approximately one quarter that of a hard automation system.

* Direct labor required for final assembly has been reduced by 20 percent.

(I) Delco Remy has been designing and manufacturing automotive electrical components for 90 years. Present product lines include batteries, starting motors, charging systems, high energy ignition systems, horns, switches, solenoids, emission control valves, sensors, permanent magnets, and vacuum actuators. In addition to nine plant locations in the United States, Delco Remy has manufacturing, sales, or engineering operations in eight countries -- France, Mexico, South Korea, England, Italy, West Germany, Luxembourg, and Japan.

Although the page numbering is clear, each page should carry also a key word identifying the story in case the pages get separated. We use to call these "slugs" in the days of line-set metal type.

"Bullets" are a good device and Steven has used these to good effect to highlight hard factual information of direct appeal to *Automation* readers.

The background on the company falls in naturally here. A summary of the importance of the story's source should always be positioned within the first few paragraphs. Perhaps Steven has gone into too long a list of products.

Page Three

The division's move toward advanced assembly systems based on robotics began in the early 1980s. At that time, (J) plans were formulated for the introduction of three major new product lines.

Management estimated that it would take $200 million in product development costs, capital expenditures, and process implementation to bring these products to market. The major problem Delco Remy faced was how to make this massive investment and still meet world-class quality, cost, and delivery standards.

"With the increasingly competitive world market, the division could not proceed in a business as usual manner," (K) said Lloyd Ford, engineering supervisor, Power Systems, with Delco Remy. "The superior versatility and repeatability of robotic systems, versus hard automation, seemed to address the manufacturing concerns of the 1980s -- high productivity and uncompromising quality.

"Plans were formulated" would be better expressed as "It planned".

Always—*always*—use direct quotes wherever possible and don't hesitate to rephrase and tighten up what was said verbatim. Of course, the source should approve the final version.

Page Four

"The reusability of robots through successive model changes presented a powerful bottom line argument in favor of adopting these systems," Ford continued. "However, we were not going to commit ourselves to making the investment in robotics until we were sure the technology met our manufacturing requirements."

(L) ROBOTICS LABORATORY

In 1982, the division formed a robotics applications laboratory.

(M)   "This laboratory represents a $1 million investment in manufacturing engineering," said Donald J. Volk, Delco Remy superintendent of Labs & Technical Services. "The goal was to create robotic systems in the lab, make sure they performed to real world conditions, and then, and only then, to move those systems into the production environment.

Subheads are as valid in media releases as they are in printed matter. They flag items of interest and provide breaks and white space in the text to improve its appearance and readability.

Quote impressive cost figures whenever you can; they give significance and perspective to any story.

Page Five

"I believe this approach is one of the principal reasons that we have been able to successfully and smoothly integrate more than 300 robots into our manufacturing operations in little more than five years -- we knew a robotic system would perform to specifications before it ever left the lab.

"Of great importance to our efforts was the assistance lent us by our corporate technical staff [AES] and suppliers, in particular GMF Robotics,"said Volk. "GMF engineers worked very closely with us in everything: integrating their RC and Karel(TM) robot controllers with our programmable logic controllers, introducing us to advanced assembly concepts, and helping us develop auxiliary robotic devices. I believe in some areas of high volume small part assembly Delco Remy and GMF broke new ground."

The quote is starting to get rather long here and should be edited more tightly.

These are details very appropriate to the specialist target audience but not to the general public.

Page Six

Volk also instituted a program of recruiting cooperative education students to work and train in the lab. When these students returned to Delco Remy as employees, they were paired with senior manufacturing engineers. These teams are credited with successfully and speedily implementing numerous robotic applications.

The first major robotic assembly system for the new product lines was released from the lab and installed at the Albany, Ga. plant in 1985. Since then two more major assembly lines have been put into production, as have many smaller systems.

The work of the laboratory continues today. At any one time six different applications are being developed. Requests for robotic systems along with production specifications come to the lab from the division's manufacturing engineers.

Here's some nice human interest stuff which could be developed for personnel and human resources publications.

Page Seven

Ⓠ The laboratory staff in conjunction with manufacturing engineers writes the software for an application, develops and "debugs" end-of-arm tooling, and makes sure the operation meets or exceeds specified cycle times and repeatability requirements before the system is released to the plant.

QUALITY

In the early 1980s, Delco Remy also launched an intensive quality improvement program. The program features extensive training in all aspects of quality improvement including statistical process control.

Machine operators are now called quality operators, which signifies their responsibility for both quality and quantity. They have been given major responsibility for seeing that their operations conform to clearly stated specifications.

Here is a source for another customized release. There are several computer magazines which would be interested in a detailed account of the writing of the software and how it relates to real-life manufacturing situations.

Page Eight

As flexible systems were about to come on line, management made a special effort to demystify robots and robotic applications for plant personnel.

"We believed it was absolutely essential to educate our work force about programmable motion devices, robots, and what these advanced machine tools could do to improve the competitive standing of the division and the quality of our products," said David M. Abel, plant manager. "I believe our people now see that the robots are helping to ensure our future."

Abel believes the 200 percent reduction in non conforming units since flexible automation went on line is directly attributable to the precision and repeatability of the robotic systems and the heightened quality awareness of the work force.

"Because of their precision, robots force you to concentrate on the production process," Abel said. "The tolerances held are so tight, sometimes as much as +/- .003 inches, that you immediately know when parts are

This is the first time that a paragraph has run over from one page to another, which should be avoided even in these days of electronic editing. Breaking paragraphs used to be forbidden when a story—particularly under the tight deadlines of a newspaper—would be split among several typesetters for keyboarding. Now it's no longer critical, but it's still a good practice. Keep the pages of copy open with lots of white space in which editors can work. This paragraph could be split after "Abel said".

Page Nine

out of conformance. The job then is to trace back through
the system to determine what is causing the problem."

(S) PRODUCTIVITY, RELIABILITY, AND FLEXIBILITY

The CS-130 alternator is one of the three new high
performance products developed during the move toward
flexible automation. (The others are a direct ignition
system and a permanent magnet gear reduction motor.)

The new alternator delivers 25 percent greater output
than its predecessor, while being both smaller and lighter.

The CS-130 final assembly line in Anderson, Ind.,
offers excellent examples of how the flexibility of robots
can be used to boost productivity, improve reliability, and
solve production problems.

The subhead is too long and is a label rather than a flag to grab interest.

Page Ten

The line features 50 GMF robots, 14 pieces of hard automation, and vision and electronic verification systems. Operations on the line are controlled through programmable logic controllers.

Fifty individual components are fed into the line, which has the capability of running 30 different models. More than 40 operations are performed. These operations include:

Ⓣ
* Palletizing/depalletizing
* Welding
* Soldering
* Fastening
* Identification stamping

* Crimping
* Seating
* Pick & place
* Insertion
* Compound application

The robots are programmed to identify the different models and to compensate as necessary.

These aren't really points to be bulleted and might be better just listed. The two-column format is difficult to cope with in most newspaper layouts.

Page Eleven

U "The ability to run 30 different models significantly enhances the efficiency of our operations," said Lloyd Ford engineering supervisor. "We are approaching just-in-time manufacturing with these systems.

"As you work with a system, you discover ways to optimize a particular operation," he continued. "You learn to move the robot more effectively and thereby cut the cycle time for that operation.

"With GMF robots you can easily make a programming change which improves reliability or solves an unexpected production problem. Hard automation generally does not present you with these kinds of fast, low cost solutions."

Ford presented the following examples:

V

PROBLEM:	Plastic pallets "curled" as components were being removed, causing alignment problems. A hard automation system would have required a costly redesign of the pallets.
SOLUTION:	Reprogram the GMF M-3 robot to remove the parts in a pattern that maintained equalized weight on the pallet.

Although *Automation's* readers will know what "just-in-time manufacturing" means, versions of this story going to less-specialist publications should include a brief explanation, which could be added to the quote without patronizing the specialist reader (e.g., by adding, "We are able to bring components to the line within a few hours of their being needed for assembly. The savings in inventory costs and space are really significant".

Breaking the text into this *problem and solution* format is a good idea; the editors at *Automation* use it as a panel. You can steer editors towards this with the latest word processing programs, which allow rules to be drawn around text.

Page Twelve

PROBLEM: Poor solder joints.

SOLUTION: Between soldering cycles, have the GMF A-1
                robot clamp the twin solder tips onto a
                copper bar, thus maintaining uniform
                temperature in each tip. Total time involved
                in making both programming and physical
                changes was four hours.

PROBLEM: Terminal head not in proper alignment.

(V) SOLUTION: Have the robot run the terminal head over a
                $ .25 steel bolt to raise it to an
                acceptable height. Total programming
                time was 30 minutes.

PROBLEM: Decreased throughput because wire leads on a
                component were being damaged as they were
                twisted together.

SOLUTION: Reprogram the robot to twist the wires in
                opposite directions. Total reprogramming time
                was 20 minutes.

PROBLEM: Line stops when castings are found to be out
                of specifications. Castings manually removed
                in anywhere from six to 90 seconds by a
                quality operator.

SOLUTION: Have the robot at the next station remove
                the casting from the line.

The spacing could be clearer. Steven correctly used double spacing between lines in his copy. I can understand why he dropped to single
spacing, with plenty of white space for editing, in these short lines. The
layout would be clearer still if there were extra spacing between each
problem and its accompanying solution.

Page Thirteen

THE FUTURE

"One robot generally does the work of two hard automation systems," Ford said. "In the future we hope to have one robot doing the work of two robots.

"This is one of the the most attractive aspects of flexible automation," he continued. "Not only do programmable devices help you work more efficiently, with greater precision, and ultimately at less cost, but also present you with the opportunity of always getting better.

"We will be moving toward even greater reliance on flexible systems as we enter the 1990s. These moves will be made as part of an overall program which emphasizes foresight and careful planning. Delco Remy is making a long term commitment to its future."

For further information on GMF robotic systems contact: The Marketing Communications Department, GMF Robotics, 2000 South Adams Road, Auburn Hills, MI 48057-2090; (313) 377-7242.

-30-

It is often difficult to know how to end a release, especially a feature.
News releases, as a rule, should be written in the form of an inverted
pyramid, with less important information coming near the end so that
it can be removed easily if space is restricted. With a feature, you need
to end strongly and forecasting future developments is a good way of
doing so. However, the quote is again getting rather long and could be
tightened up. Stylistically, it's not a good idea to try to do this just by
putting in phrases like "he continued" or "he emphasized", but by careful
editing.

It is always worth putting in contact details for the company or client at
the end of a story as part of the text. Lots of specialist magazines give
these details as a service to readers, not just a plug. When possible, name
a specific person as the contact, as well as, or instead of, the department.

Steven has used the "-30-" journalistic convention to indicate the end of
the piece, which helps to identify him as a pro. Just "End" or "Ends" is
more usual internationally.

Did you ever wonder why Sotheby's, the auctioneering firm, gets so much media coverage, even when they are not selling multimillion-dollar Impressionist paintings? The answer is a steady flow of well-written news releases backed up by excellent photographs, such as this Kashan Tree of Life Prayer Rug sold at auction for a comparatively modest $6,000. The picture, when accompanied by a release giving its background, has sufficient interest to generate wide editorial coverage.

The Power of Posters
Restrooms are an unexploited medium

That wonderful communications medium—the poster—is a sadly neglected PR tool. In the movie industry, we always have a provision for posters written into a program for a new film launch, but that discipline is imposed by the needs of theaters to have display materials.

Live-performance and movie theaters—both four-wallers and drive-ins—have opportunities for promotional displays that point to much wider applications of posters to get a message across. Above all, don't think of posters as a straight advertising medium—they also can be valid for messages being communicated with "below-the-line" PR activities.

I got very good results in movies with "miniposters", in other words, fliers. The flier or handbill is really a poster that is circulated rather than put up in a prominent position as a display item. The standard American 8½-inch by 11-inch letter page, the Metric equivalent A4 sheet, or something somewhat bigger—legal or ledger (A3 metric) size—gives you room for visuals with impact and for a lot of written information, if you really need to say a lot to communicate effectively.

THE LAVATORIAL MEDIUM

All these page sizes fit well in places in which conventional, larger posters are just not appropriate. I got considerable impact with a movie promotion in which miniposters were pinned on the back of lavatory doors throughout a chain of over 200 theaters. Nowhere else can you communicate to such a captive audience! A few—but not enough—internal communicators in corporations and other organizations use their restrooms as a place to display messages aimed at employees. I think every corporate PR practitioner should look at this by no means flippant suggestion as a way of promulgating to the workforce highlights of an annual report, a new employee benefits scheme, or similar information.

Airlines miss a great opportunity by not putting miniposters in aircraft restrooms. Before we move on from the comfort stop medium, consider also adhesive patches with strong simple messages for restroom mirrors and walls.

STICKERS PUSH THE MESSAGE

When I launched a not very good—but quite funny—movie called *Crazy People,* I blitzed restrooms with little circular stickers in yellow with a smiling face printed on them—the logostyle for the film. It was difficult to visit a public restroom in town without seeing this logo, and I am sure it contributed very cost-effectively to creating awareness of the picture and generating healthy box office revenues before that most powerful communications medium of all—word of mouth—spread that it really wasn't worth seeing.

Adhesive stickers work particularly well with kids and for reminder messages for all ages—as done very effectively by the American Heart Association and other organizations in kick-smoking kits. If you are promoting a "Say No to Drugs", dental hygiene awareness, or other message to the young, consider the humble sticker, print a lot of them, and get them out there working for you. If the design is trendy and eye-catching, the kids will plaster them everywhere—on themselves, their clothes, their school bags, their lunchboxes, their books, their cars—all over.

Stimulate Word of Mouth

Stickers aimed at kids worked particularly well for me for the first *Star Wars* movie, when I ordered thousands proclaiming simply "May The Force Be with You". My timing was right because I got the stickers out early to exploit the strongly positive advance word-of-mouth publicity about *Star Wars* before it went on general release.

There is one sticker that illustrates how long-lasting, repetitive and effective a medium this can be. It is located in a bottom corner of the windscreen on my Ford Taurus and tells me in a stylish way that the car was built with pride by both workers and management at the Chicago plant. It somehow gives me a warm feeling every time I see it, although the reaction could be strongly negative if the car proves to be unreliable or reveals annoying defects!

But back to posters.

USE VOLUNTEERS

Don't leave the poster to the advertising fraternity; instead, use it wherever possible in your media mix. If you have a message that is in the public interest, you are likely to generate more sympathy and cooperation in getting permission to display it. The French, Germans and other Europeans have some lessons for us in the use of the poster and flier, their traditional communications tools. Small groups with a message to get across with a limited budget will run off perhaps just a few hundred small posters and put them up all over a neighborhood or even a town. You can extend the distribution nationally if your organization has local groups of volunteers.

Some municipalities are quite tolerant of noncommercial poster sticking and will not strictly enforce local laws. Don't abuse the privilege, though, and always, as soon as possible after the event or campaign you are promoting is over, remove your posters from places they are not supposed to be—on trees and lamp posts, for example. That's not only considerate to the environment and the community but also obviates the negative image that is associated with an outdated poster becoming shabby and an environmental eyesore.

If you create the standard miniposter or full-size poster, don't think that those formats are the limits of the scale of display you can create. The movie distributors have departments that can do incredible things with posters, especially those with strong visuals.

JUMBO DISPLAYS ARE EASY

There is a very old device called the *epidiascope,* now sold primarily through commercial art stores, which enables the layman to make impressive giant displays. You put the artwork—perhaps a section of a poster—underneath the epidiascope, which can project a large image onto a big sheet of paper or Styrofoam, or even a wall. Very little artistic skill is needed to draw the outlines and fill in the coloring and shading of the enlarged image. If you project onto Styrofoam, cardboard, or building board, you can create cut-out figures and logos that can make dramatic displays.

You can also do blowups by photographing artwork with an ordinary 35mm camera using color slide film and projecting the image through a standard 35mm projector. A cheaper alternative with a faster turnaround in the film processing is to shoot a high-contrast negative on color print film, put the negative into a slide mount, and project that, but the image will not be very clear and you may have difficulty picking out detail.

BE IMAGINATIVE

Be as imaginative with your posters as you are with your other communications media. The Concerned American Indian Parents were featured in *Fortune* magazine with a story about their 1,000 posters, which used pennants for fictitious sports teams to drive home their message against racism.

The Minneapolis-based pressure group deliberately set out to provoke people and so increase awareness of the racism issue. Their posters for such fictitious teams as the San Diego Caucasians and the Kansas City Jews underlined their protest against the implicit racism they perceived in names like the Cleveland Indians, the Washington Redskins, the Atlanta Braves and the Kansas City Chiefs.

Political posters cry out for some imaginative treatment, but I still think the biggest area for proper exploitation of the poster medium is internal PR to promulgate information to employees in their work, eating, and recreation areas. I've seen some good examples of this in the small rest areas in Japanese manufacturing plants; in factories all over the world, you will find these areas, with beverage machines and seats. Often it is here that quality-control and similar workers' groups meet, so these are highly visible places in which to display posters.

DON'T PATRONIZE OR BE AGGRESSIVE

But be careful that posters do not communicate a corporate message in an aggressive or patronizing way, which might generate adverse reactions. You are actually invading the personal space of employees when you take your message into areas intended for them to treat as their own. Whatever you do must be sympathetic to the attitudes of your target audience.

You would, for example, use the employee poster medium to keep the workforce informed about progress in a takeover or merger situation or for details of a new employee benefit scheme, but definitely not to promulgate management views during the delicate period of a labor dispute.

Use Nostalgia to Strengthen Your Message
Dove Bars and Goodyear show how

Nostalgia is always a great peg (or hook) on which to hang a PR message. I particularly like the way that Dove Bar launched its vending-cart service in New York. The distribution of samples was tied in to the fact that New York was where the founder of the company, Leo Stefanos, first arrived in America from Greece. His son Mike described it to *Entrepreneur* magazine as a gesture of "giving something back to New York from my dad"—a nice warm promotional touch that contributed to over a million Dove Bar sales from vending carts in the city in the first season.

Nostalgia works at any level, and you can often deploy it when your own message does not have a particularly strong communication value.

EXPLOIT PERSONAL INTERESTS

Vince Walsh of New Jersey has provided me with a nice example of how you can grab attention by zeroing in on an area of personal interest in your target audience, even if that area is far removed from the products or services you are offering. When Vince launched his Princeton Desktop Publishing Company, he needed to demonstrate to clients that processing copy and layouts on a Macintosh computer could give good results. He prepared an attractive layout on his Mac, featuring one of his most successful photographs, which reeked of baseball nostaliga. The picture shows Brooklyn Dodger bullpen action before the top of the ninth inning in one of the last games played at Ebbets Field, Brooklyn, in 1957.

The simple, two-color folder has a quiz and background information of great appeal to all baseball fans and demonstrates the merits of desktop layout and typography. It is a natural lead-in to Vince's corporate brochure, which details his expertise and the services he can provide to newsletter publishers and other clients.

"Top of the 9th"
Ebbets Field, Brooklyn
August 25, 1957

Photography by Vince Walsh

This historic color photograph, reproduced here in black and white, shows bullpen action before the top of the ninth inning in one of the last games played at Ebbets Field, Brooklyn, August 25, 1957.

Do you know who the five Brooklyn Dodgers in the photo are? See inside for answers.

Research assistance by:
**Clifford Kachline, Society for American Baseball Research and Baseball Hall of Fame Library
Cooperstown, New York**

Photo and Text Copyright © 1987 Princeton Desktop Publishing

This is the desktop published brochure that Vince Walsh uses so effectively as a publicity tool exploiting nostalgia and the national interest in baseball. The brochure is a very soft sell describing the game action and the historic significance of the photo "Top of the 9th", which features Sandy Koufax early in his career before he went on to become a baseball legend with 165 career victories.

ANNIVERSARIES PROVIDE A PEG

Extending the nostalgia peg further, seek anniversaries or other appropriate dates on which to hang a PR program. Among my essential reference books are those listing anniversaries, but make sure you use one with a reputation for accuracy. Scan through the dates that fit in with the timing of your promotion to see if there is an anniversary that you can tie into.

As I write this, I'm thinking about an animal welfare promotion, and in the reference books I find the feast of St. Francis of Assisi on October 4. I might make something of February 23, when Leo Hendrik Baekeland (the inventor of Bakelite) died, for a new plastics product; January 28, the birthday of William Seward Burroughs (inventor of the first popular adding machine) for a computer product; or April 7, the anniversary of the founding of the World Health Organization, for a pharmaceutical product.

I have found anniversaries particularly good pegs on which to hang the rerelease of old movies. Even if anniversaries are not of sufficient significance to merit inclusion in an advertising campaign, they often can give greater editorial credibility to a feature story with PR objectives.

For example, a client wishing to promote a psychiatric-services practice and holding an open workshop on self-hypnosis stands a better chance of getting media coverage if the workshop is timed for May 6, the birthday of Sigmund Freud, the founder of psychoanalysis. You then have a peg on which to hang a local media feature about the developments in psychiatry; the media will have no problem including the fact that the client will review this subject at his or her function.

DIG INTO THE ARCHIVES

Often with new clients, I probe their archives looking for corporate anniversaries that I can "celebrate" to give extra impact to both internal and external PR efforts. This has worked very well with motor companies, because they have anniversaries of model family launches, plant openings, and the introduction of major technological developments, which can be built into features and pictures to appeal to both specialist magazines and local media.

You must beware, though, of overkill in this, as in everything in PR. Don't try to build an event into a major effort unless it has the significance to justify it.

Additionally, there are a number of PR case histories that have worked very well without a specific anniversary peg but that dug back into nostalgia to position a new product in relation to its tried and proven predecessors.

You may battle to get a picture about a new product published because it is so obviously a plug, but if you show it with earlier examples and write an editorially attractive caption about how the design and features have developed, you have something with intrinsic reader interest that better merits publication.

INGENIOUS LINKS

When the wreckage of a vintage airplane was discovered in Antarctica in 1988, Goodyear leaped into the topical nostalgia window with a story and picture of a snow cruiser ground vehicle that met a similar fate when it was abandoned in the Antarctic nearly 50 years ago. This was a good example of a media release exploiting nostalgia.

The release and caption used ingenious links to plug Goodyear's image and products.

The introduction was rather soft, but this was not a news story, and there was an impact word, "wreckage", right at the beginning. Incidentally, I had an editor in my early journalistic days who maintained that it was bad policy to start newspaper stories with the definite article, especially in the era when every story was set with an initial drop letter. "Starting with 'the' is the easy way, and if everybody does it you get a page littered with Ts," he said, furious because just that had happened with the front page he was waving in front of me.

Creating a story and getting a picture published by exploiting both nostalgia and topical news pegs are principles typified in the distribution by Goodyear of an archival print of the Penguin Antarctic vehicle from 1940. There are frequent opportunities to generate fresh exposure for file pictures.

START WITH IMPACT

"Try to hit off with an impact word that grabs attention, not the definite—nor indefinite article either or we risk getting 'As' all over the place."

Although newspapers tend not to use many drop letters any more, the initial word in each piece is usually at least set in caps and prominent. Get an impact word in there right at the start, but don't be such a slave to the rule that, just to avoid starting with 'the' or 'a', introductory sentences become tortuous.

The Goodyear release started with an impact phrase to get the topical peg right up front, and was followed by two paragraphs of backup facts, leading into a quote that gently and logically brought in the Goodyear name.

A quote was included from the curator of the World of Rubber exhibit, not identified as a company man, although the exhibit was stated to be located at Goodyear's headquarters. This is sourcing that is appropriate, authoritative, and subtle, all at the same time.

SOFT SELL

Beginning with the second paragraph inherently interesting facts and figures were presented that communicated—without directly plugging—the rubber company's scale of operations—"the 300 millionth tire"—and technological strengths. Then came more interesting background and an ingenious twist at the end bringing Goodyear's dirigible business into the act as well. It was a tenuous link, but still credible.

There was really nothing of topical substance in this story—it was imaginatively contrived. Yet no journalist could have complained that it was valueless "junk mail" that deserved to go straight into the circular file. Instead, clever and justified use gave a new lease of life to archive material.

The picture was, as always with Goodyear's media photographs, well-composed and professionally processed.

PICTURE AND CAPTION POINTERS

You would think in these high tech days that any company or PR agency would automatically release only photographs with the right range of contrast, properly exposed and focused on glossy stock with an easily removed caption fastened to the back.

Don't believe it! A disturbing proportion of publicity photographs break one or more of these rules, particularly the one about the caption. Captions should always be fastened to pictures, so that the words and the visual stay together as far as the editor's desk. Then they need to be easy-to-separate, because the caption will go to one place to be edited and keyboarded, the photograph to another to be processed. Before it leaves the editorial department, the photograph must be cropped and scaled, which is done usually on the reverse side over a light box using a crayon or grease pencil to mark the area to be reproduced. That's why the caption needs to pull cleanly away, leaving a clear reverse side for scaling and cropping marks and instructions to the production department.

Pay attention to the way the release is set out. There is room for some criticism in the Goodyear example. It was packed too tightly on the page and would have benefited by a deeper top border with a heading and a *slug* (an identifying word). It would have been more attractive and easier to read if there had been extra space between the paragraphs, a cross heading or subheading every three or four paragraphs, and a date somewhere.

TO DATE OR NOT TO DATE

There are differing opinions about dating releases, especially because the postal service is so erratic and delays happen often. One school of thought says that if you date a release, it will have a shorter life, as editors tend not to keep even a relatively timeless story like this one, because it soon appears to be stale if the date is prominent. Another school maintains that everything should be dated to help the media people, and that it is not really ethical to omit the date in the hope that a story or picture is more likely to be used later, perhaps in the erroneous belief that it has only recently been issued. This school believes that editors—and writers, generally—are notoriously untidy, hoard things and, when there is a hole in a page, ferret in their drawers for something to fill it.

DANGERS OF DATING

I tend to use a date only when it really is important for the journalist to know the date, especially because much of my material circulates internationally and I never know when it might arrive in Melbourne, Bombay, or Ougadougou.

I certainly did not date one of my longest-running photo releases. Taking my kids to a wildlife park on a cold winter's day, we were amused to see a group of baboons sitting like gossiping old men around a log fire that the keepers had built for them. On the next day I was back with a photographer to show the group around the fire with, in the background but very much in focus, two car models

I was publicizing. That picture must have gone into lots of editorial drawers, because it kept resurfacing in the strangest publications during subsequent winters. If I'd dated it, I'm sure it would not have had such a long life.

Deal with the Details
Successful author shows how

Confidence, determination and the ability to attend to all the details are key elements in even the most modest PR campaign. They are exemplified in a publisher's dream of a PR-oriented author, Judith Briles, who has personally hustled many of her books onto the best seller list.

In fact, all Judith's books should be subtitled "she did it her way", because she has single-handedly generated more publicity for them than her publishers could achieve. For example, her *Woman to Woman* was, she says, "being treated with benign regret" until, in frustration, she got out in the marketplace and hustled it with good, basic PR techniques.

"I have taken over all my own PR for my books, because if I don't demonstrate my belief in them, how can I expect anyone else to," she told me. "But it's hard work."

RESEARCH YOUR TARGETS

"I used to be a stockbroker, so I knew very little about PR—but I did know about sources for information and how to research.

"My first PR action was to get a copy of *Literary Market Place* and used it to identify the publications and television and radio stations through which I wanted to generate publicity.

"Then, before I got on the telephone and personally called around to producers and editors, I developed a publicity hook for the book I was promoting. This is a simple angle which is topical and high in human interest. For *Woman to Woman* it was the proposition that the typical man does not just discriminate against women—he discriminates against everybody!"

That provocative concept took Judith onto national television on the *Oprah Winfrey, Donahue, Hour Magazine,* and other television shows and into the pages of publications from *Time* to *People* to *The National Enquirer*—and all those in between. She got four pages in

People by her own efforts seven months after her book was published. That shows that by determined PR you can maintain visibility. It is not just what is *new* that makes news.

"It is very important to follow up with appreciative letters,"
emphasizes Judith. "I always sent a letter of thanks to producers,
interviewers and others involved with shows on which I appeared.
I even thanked interviewers who were so rude and hostile that I
vowed never to go on their shows again—but I wrote 'jerk' on the
file copies just to remind me."

SEEKING COMPATIBLE PERSONALITIES

This points to the important fact that PR people who organize
television and radio appearances must keep in mind the personality
of the person they are promoting and try to get a good match
between interviewer and interviewee.

"If you have the flair and determination, you are always your
own best PR representative," says Judith. "What really counts after
you have the opportunity to appear in a program is how you come
across before the cameras or the microphones."

I have seen some of Judith's many media releases and the important lesson they reveal is that the simple, clear approach always
works best. One of her publishers produced a very literate and highly
detailed long news release about one of her books that generated
very little editorial exposure. When Judith took over her own PR
she produced a release on the same subject that is brief, tight, and
to-the-point and concentrates on clearly communicating a few basic
ideas.

She proves that KISS—"Keep It Simple, Stupid"—works.

FAILURE TO RESEARCH THE MEDIA

Judith's preliminary research into the media and their needs is a
lesson that many professional PR practitioners would do well to heed
before they start spending their clients' money.

There is no excuse for anyone in the marketing communications
business to be unaware of both the technical and the editorial con-

tent needs of any major publication. Yet often they are not sensitive to the requirements of even the most important potential outlets for their material. Reporters for the leading national newspaper in the United States, *USA Today,* tell me that even the largest—and presumably most knowledgeable—PR consultancies continually inundate them with outdated, totally unsuitable material, much of it badly written and reflecting no attempt to meet the paper's style or other requirements.

"They don't seem to know either our deadlines or our basic editorial philosophies," reporter Pat Guy told me. "We all tend to get angry at the mass of really stupid stuff sent to us, most of which goes straight into the trash can at great cost to their clients.

"Of course, some public relations people really know their jobs—and our needs. But the industry generally does not do a good job—even with its own PR."

I have found that attitude very prevalent among journalists all over the world. Aside from getting our clients' releases used more widely, we need to project greater professionalism toward journalists if we are to attract more of the better ones to make career moves and bring their talents to our profession.

Digital Shows How to Stage the Big Event
Serving the media's needs

Exhibitions and similar trade events can be powerful PR tools, but they risk becoming *passé* and purely commercial in the eyes of reporters, so one of the biggest problems is to get good media attendance and coverage.

Burson-Marsteller, the world's biggest PR consultancy, and Digital Equipment Corporation teamed up to do an imaginative job of tackling these problems for the 1987 DECWORLD, Digital's annual trade exhibition. It illustrates very effectively how to protect a company that could be vulnerable to reporters seeking negative angles to prick a bubble of consistent success.

There was no doubt about Digital's success after two years of peak performance and outsmarting industry leader IBM. The agency was aware of this when it conducted media audits, which revealed also that DECWORLD 1987 had to promise good copy if the media were to turn out in force.

INTEGRATE—BUT DISTINGUISH PR FROM COMMERCIAL OBJECTIVES

The planning by the special PR task force created for the project began eight months before the event, when they set out to decide how to deploy their $200,000 budget.

The integration of the PR needs with the more directly sales-oriented objectives of the exhibition enabled PR to be designed into the whole event without compromising the sales effort. The media perceived it to be a function conceived very much for their specific needs, especially because the agency identified nine media groups with common editorial interests and so customized both events and stories to address these editorial interests specifically.

For example, to get the *Wall Street Journal* and *Business Week* to attend your show out of the many to which their representatives are invited, you must set up situations that they know will generate good copy. It can be self-defeating to lump such premier business journals together with the editors of obscure technological publications. DECWORLD *did* attract both categories; over 500 editors from all the target media attended, and 500 stories were printed in 300 publications around the world as a result of their differing and individual requirements having been met during the same event.

Much of this success was achieved by setting up a series of interviews with Digital senior executives and matching executives and the media according to their specialities. There was additional face-to-face communication of Digital's message to target media through an open forum featuring the company's vice-presidents.

It is always important to cater to the special needs of electronic media representatives—both to make their jobs easier and to avoid any clash with print media people who often feel that events are dominated by the demands and status of the television crews. DEC-WORLD generated nearly an hour of broadcast time—3½ times that of the previous year—on over 30 local, network and cable stations in the United States.

EMPHASIZE SCALE

It can be particularly difficult to meet a PR objective that requires a strong message of a company's global strengths. The United States media tend to be very parochial, but they could not fail to get—and communicate to the target audiences—the message that Digital is a big, *international* operation. DECWORLD opened with the plugging in, on the exhibit floor, of the largest private nondefense computer network in the world. It was an event with strong intrinsic news value and positioned the company as being at the vanguard of global computer networking.

The international connections were emphasized—and great opportunities for photographs were created—by using the cruise ship *Queen Elizabeth II* for additional hotel and conference space. The giant ship was not just there—it made a grand entrance into Boston harbor.

Scale and impact need not cost a lot of money if you seek out alternatives. I found I could hire these guardsmen to provide music and give an extra impetus to a promotion I staged in London at less than the cost to engage an ordinary dance band. Part of the deal was the requirement to announce that they "appeared by kind permission of Her Majesty the Queen". That was no problem— I emphasized it, and overseas media representatives seemed particularly impressed that we could actually get the sovereign's cooperation for our publicity efforts!

TIME PRODUCT ANNOUNCEMENTS CAREFULLY

The media representatives were brought into contact with Digital's customers to get their views; many companies lack the confidence or perception to see the value of this.

If you are asking, "What about the products?"—they were not forgotten. There were 26 new product announcements at the show to add to its impact and to give further ammunition for media coverage. However, there are many situations in which this might not be a wise tactic, and media coverage could be increased and the visibility of a company maintained more easily over an extended period of time by staggering product announcements.

It need not take much to turn an otherwise routine event into a great PR vehicle. When Ford of Europe hosted a banquet honoring world champion Jackie Stewart's retirement from motor racing, the photographers expected to get only the usual society shots of happy people drinking, eating, and dancing. But when Jackie, followed by Princess Anne and his wife Helen, entered the ballroom, he found all the guests wearing his trademark, cloth caps and sunglasses. The photographers blazed away and the event was publicized internationally just because of this imaginative gimmick.

If there is one prime lesson to be learned from this outstanding PR exercise, it is that, even with a program on the grandest of scales, it is still vital to customize its elements to cater to specific media interests. The stories and activities must focus on each of the target media groups.

Don't try a "scatter-shot" approach in the hope that general material will hit all your objectives effectively. Media material must be sorted and prepackaged to be appropriate to the individual reporter and editor. That is where a preliminary audit of strategic media interests and attitudes can prove so valuable.

The Logistical Problems of a PR Event
They are always worse than you expect

If you undertake a complex publicity event, expect the logistics and complications to be far worse than you can anticipate. Keep bubbling with enthusiasm, though, or you will fail to motivate the rest of your team (and anybody else whose cooperation you need to make it a success).

Those are key lessons New York marketing consultant Dean Fox learned the hard way when he pulled off an amazing stunt. It culminated with Dean walking four blocks down Sixth Avenue on a curb-to-curb carpet, rubbing shoulders with one of the greatest galaxies of show biz stars ever assembled anywhere.

The aspect of this case history that really appeals to me is the attention to detail Dean paid when he coordinated this remarkable event. It went right through to a novel followup that kept the publicity flowing indefinitely. When the New York carpet trodden on by the stars was taken up, it was sliced into 6-inch squares and sent to the client's prime target audience as collectible keepsakes. Nice touch.

BOOSTING MARKET SHARE

The client was Allied Signal, trading then as Allied Chemicals and taking on Dupont to get a bigger share of the market for synthetic carpet fibers. At the time, Allied was spending about $2 million per year on advertising this area of activity, so it was a radical departure for them to put even more into a one-night grand slam to achieve maximum impact. But it paid off: they gained ten points in market share in a month.

Dean worked closely with that doyen of Broadway theatrical producers Alexander Cohen, who was producing the Night of a Hundred Stars benefit for the Actors' Fund. Dean's client was only one of six sponsors of the ABC Network special, but this clever promotion allowed them to get the greatest impact for their money.

GIANT RED CARPET

Sixth Avenue was covered curb-to-curb for four blocks with a rich red carpet patterned with stars. That mammoth undertaking cost around $500,000 (partly because some of New York's notorious pot-holes needed to be filled in before the carpet could be glued to the road surface). After the show was videotaped at Radio City, the stars walked down the carpet to a reception at the Hilton Hotel.

Large crowds lined the streets to watch and the media coverage was great—with the carpet featuring prominently, of course.

"The planning took six months, and there were numerous difficulties," Dean recalled. "I think the most important lesson about PR I learned was the need to maintain your enthusiasm. We had endless meetings with local authorities, and it was largely our enthusiasm which kept them motivated and helping us to do all the things that were required. Alex Cohen really taught me that almost anything is possible if you approach it with enthusiasm."

EXPLOITING STAR CELEBRITIES

The really attractive aspect of this promotion is how the stars of a glittering showbiz event were put to such good promotional use. The big picture for all the media was the celebrities right on top of the client's product. It couldn't lose. Stars are usually very expensive, and you must leverage their publicity value as much as possible to get a good return on your dollars.

Also, when using star talent, make your prime targets feel like part of the action. Allied flew in 80 mill owners and sat them in $1,000 seats; their subsequent walk down the Sixth Avenue carpet with the stars must be something that even the most jaded among them will always remember and associate with the company in a warm way.

Incidentally, I once worked for a big company executive reputed to have been seen strolling along the waterfront in Monte Carlo with Princess Grace on one arm and Elizabeth Taylor on the other. Whether it was true or not, I never investigated, because it had become part of the corporate folklore and did powerful PR for him within the company!

Drama as a Medium to Increase Audience Participation
A novel Canadian program

It is sad that gatherings of public relations people often tend to be rather boring, mutual ego-stroking sessions. A notable exception was the imaginative event staged by the Canada Division of the San Francisco–based International Association of Business Communicators to get members really thinking about a new professional code of ethics for which their input was required.

The association chose a novel and memorable way of making its members examine the issues of professional ethics and personal moral values. These frequently conflict, so the IABC used drama as a vehicle to get members participating in an exchange of views on how this conflict is best managed.

This case history offers many lessons and will suggest how drama can be used as a lively, high-impact, participatory medium for PR, especially when a target audience is already being brought together for a conference or some other meeting.

ONE-ACT PLAY

The IABC production was a one-act play set in a courtroom and presented during the Canada Division's annual conference. A freelance writer created the script in which a communicator was put on trial for her actions during a corporate crisis. The audience was sworn in as the jury with the task of assessing the guilt or innocence of the communicator failing to give out information in violation of her professional ethics.

It was a tough call because, if she did talk to the media, she risked jeopardizing the development of a cure for cancer.

LINKING IN VIDEO

The "evidence" was introduced to the audience in the form of a television newscast on video, a useful device to convey information in an attractive form and give a sense of immediacy. The ensuing dramatic production raised three basic ethical questions for PR people:

- What does the public have a right to know during a crisis?
- What responsibility does the communicator have to the public and to his or her employer?
- Does the government, as a regulator and investor, have any special obligations during a crisis?

The audience/jury split into groups after the drama, each with a foreperson who had attended prior orientation briefings. They were given only 45 minutes to reach their conclusions, and this time pressure helped to stimulate lively and unrestrained discussions.

The presentation was followed up five weeks later with a questionnaire, to which over 50 percent of delegates responded, a very good indication of the high interest the drama had generated. Not only that, the responses indicated that the information conveyed in the drama had been well-retained and had stimulated considerable constructive thought about the association's Code of Ethics. Delegates were enthusiastic about this unusual PR approach, awarding the drama a score of 329 out of a possible 345 points for its excellence, well in excess of any other sessions at the conference.

Theatrical productions have become quite commonplace at marketing and sales gatherings but do not figure prominently in PR activities. This Canadian venture demonstrated their potential, particularly if there can be full audience participation.

PROFESSIONAL AND AMATEUR VOLUNTEERS

The Canadians used professionals who volunteered their services for much of the production. Most organizations can draw on accomplished amateurs who will participate willingly in this kind of venture from within their own group or from the local community.

You do not need to go to the complexity of a fictional dramatic production to stage a live, participatory event with a touch of showmanship. The best "open house" and media tour functions I have attended have been staged to make the client's staff play their own real-life roles and interact with the audience of visitors in an entertaining and meaningful way.

Research and development facilities are ideal for this kind of approach. Get the staff to set up interesting experiments or testing procedures; the visitors tour the various locations, watching and asking questions. Always have a summarized fact sheet at each location explaining what is going on.

A similar approach can be adopted for plant tours, with the different job functions demonstrated in the same way.

REHEARSALS ESSENTIAL

It is essential to rehearse the program, especially when you are involving staff who are not used to dealing with the media. Get someone to play the role of the most demanding visitor you can expect to get. An automotive manufacturer, before a tour of its new test track and engineering laboratory facilities, asked me to rehearse the tour as an aggressive, difficult journalist asking awkward questions and not being satisfied with inadequate answers.

The engineers on duty said afterwards that they found it a very challenging situation and my attitude made it difficult at first for them not to respond in a hostile way. It prepared them well to cope with the media representatives who flew in the next day and the tour went off without a hitch.

You can increase the degree of audience participation by linking a tour with a quiz or series of tests, with prizes awarded afterwards for the best scores. Make the quiz or tests fun so that they are an enjoyable experience, and avoid anything that will embarrass those who do not do well.

MAKE EVERYONE FEEL LIKE A VIP

Convey to your visitors the impression that they are privileged and are getting a really full inside view of your activities. Show that you trust them and are holding nothing back. That means making sure that any products or processes you do not want them to see for security reasons are discreetly excluded from the tour.

When I visited a Japanese manufacturing plant and research facility once, my hosts went out of their way to emphasize that it was an unrestricted, behind-the-scenes view of their activities. However, at a number of locations, temporary screens had been erected with prominent "Restricted Area—No Entry" signs posted, which rather spoiled the overall impression my hosts were trying to create for their PR purposes. I felt denied access to the most interesting material, not trusted enough to share their secrets.

There might be situations in which you want to create the impression of a lot of secret, very important work going on in a facility, but you must handle these with great sensitivity to avoid the possibly negative reactions of visitors you are trying to impress.

PARTICIPATION IS THE KEY

Participation should be a key word in any PR event, because making your target audience feel involved is an important way of generating enthusiasm and making your message more memorable. It need not be complicated; often the simplest participatory actions can be amazingly effective in communicating the information you need to get across.

I found this when I worked with a group called in to tackle the problem of Africans operating engine-powered farm equipment for the first time. Conventional training techniques had failed to make them comprehend the importance of basic maintenance procedures, notably the necessity in their dusty environment of cleaning engine air filters every day.

Diagrams, films, slide shows and lectures failed to work. Our solution was very simple. We took air filter housings and fastened plastic tubes to them. We explained to the tribespeople that engines, like humans and animals, need to breathe. Then we got them to breathe themselves through the plastic piping, first with clean and then with clogged air filters in place. They got the message immediately.

DON'T BE AFRAID TO BE NAIVE

Does that sound too naive an approach to be applicable to more sophisticated audiences? Don't you believe it! One of the best pieces of advice I received early in my career was when I prepared a package of material for a very high level business target audience. The chairman of the client company rejected it as being far too complex for his counterparts.

In writing or any other communications activity, simplicity and clarity are all important. You rarely succeed if one motivation is to try to impress your target audience with your own sophistication and literary skills.

The people who understand this best are those most successful in publishing for the business community, because they know that their often very up-market audiences still want information expressed as simply and effectively as possible without the need to work hard to understand it. The words must be in common usage (except for technical phrases familiar to your target audience), the sentences short, and the phrasing simple and direct with a logical progression of information, ideas, and any background necessary for easy comprehension.

THE FOG INDEX

You can assess your written material for these qualities by using the Fog Index, which is a measure of the number of years of education required to read and understand copy without difficulty.

You get the Fog index rating by adding up two prime factors in your copy:

1. The average number of words in a sentence.
2. The average of three-syllable words in every 100 words of copy.

Add the two totals and then multiply by 0.4 to get the Fog Index of the number of years of education required to read the copy easily.

Our most successful publications—the leading newspapers, including the businessman's bible *The Wall Street Journal* and other magazines—score around 10 or 11. You do not even need to be a high school graduate to understand them, although their target audiences may have much higher literacy levels.

My first submission of copy to that chairman was, I thought, a great literary effort that would impress him and his high-level clients.

It had a Fog Index of around 20, not quite as bad as Milton's *Paradise Lost*, which scores 26, but almost as difficult to comprehend quickly and totally inappropriate for our communications objectives. My second draft came in around 10, the same as the beautifully written Gettysburg Address—a PR classic in its own right!

With any PR, cut out what's superfluous and don't try to impress. The ability to communicate in the most effective way is the paramount requirement. Aim for elegant simplicity.

Rent-a-Writer to Get the Publicity Flowing

An outside perspective generates new PR ammunition

One of the most cost-effective actions organizations of almost any size can take to generate editorial promotional material is to appoint a "writer-at-large." It is such an obvious and effective step that it is amazing so few companies do this—especially those employing PR agencies at high cost for comparatively little creative output.

When I have acted as PR consultant for the agencies or subsidiaries of big multinational companies, I have frequently been appalled at how little imaginative and publishable editorial material originates from the central PR department. It has enabled *me* to make a lot of money creating that material as a consultant/writer.

This is a great area of PR in which to specialize, because, if you have the appropriate skills and experience, it can be very easy and can impress the clients greatly. Much of the raw material for good publicity comes from asking questions and from sifting through the mass of non-PR documentation in the technical and training material generated about new products, processes, or market trends.

Already published sources can be grist to the corporate writer's mill. Tap into those wonderful new computerized data bases with a few well-chosen key words, or spend an hour or two in the nearest public library. Invest a hundred dollars or so in one of those portable copiers that you can run over the page of an interesting reference to make the note-taking much faster and more comprehensive.

LIBRARY RESEARCH PAYS OFF

I wrote the equivalent of a full-length novel to launch a major movie in a national market mainly from library research of existing material. The press kit that came with the film was impressive in size and obviously had been expensive to print and package. The stories, though, were dull and notably lacking in the human-interest angles that a journalist would have identified and covered.

I have created press kits for launches of cars and other consumer products by jettisoning much of what the central PR department produced and interviewing engineers, service people and customers and plundering training manuals and other technical documentation to get meatier material.

You do not need to be brilliant at finding angles and stories to generate media coverage at a variety of levels. Just be prepared to approach the publicity needs *from the viewpoint of the media and their readers,* get out a notebook, dig for information, and then hit the word processor.

THE ROLE OF THE COMPETENT HACK

For too many PR people, producing simple, punchy editorial is regarded as hack work. I've heard numerous negative comments in the profession from communications and publicity specialists who have not been through the journalistic mill about the "let's find the angles and churn out the copy" approach to publicity. Writing PRs sometimes seems to be regarded as having a form of professional expertise inferior to that of PR people who create spectacular promotions or sparkle with ideas at meetings.

I'm proud of being a competent hack, and most organizations would benefit from having one at their disposal—the *writer-at-large* (a label preferable to the more usual, academic *writer-in-residence* because writers can be inhibited by being part of the action rather than observers of it).

When I joined Ford in Europe, PR chief Walter Hayes was adamant in his instructions that I should stay well away from all the time-consuming meetings and other in-house activities that take up such a large portion of a manager's day

Big organizations generate a great deal of internal activity by their personnel, especially at management levels. A PR staff member may expend as much effort on housekeeping duties to maintain and service the structure of the organization, as on producing communications materials to market goods, services and images externally.

This whittles away drastically at the amount of time and energy that should be directed at pursuing the organization's interests to generate bottom-line profits from positive exposure. Protect your

Press pictures must be visually interesting in a way that emphasizes the PR message you are trying to get across. Two of the features I needed to promote for this new car were the large rear hatch and the amount of internal space, both improvements over the previous model. So I set the inside up as a mini-office and used a model to create an interesting shot that conveyed the image of space and load-carrying versatility. This shot was used extensively all over the world.

writer from all those corporate duties. An in-house PR can find it very difficult to be really productive in the generation of media releases, which often get put aside while he tackles the seemingly more important and time-sensitive in-house corporate demands.

WORDS TO SUPPORT AN IMAGE CHANGE

Walter Hayes of Ford knew this. His idea was to exploit my international writing background and generate a steady flow of editorial material that would support the change of image—from a producer of stodgy, unenterprising engineering for the masses to an innovative manufacturer of more exciting, sporty, and trendy cars and trucks—necessary for Ford to cope with shifts in the marketplace.

In effect, I was a writer-at-large, almost a free-lance writer, although a full-time employee with office, secretary, and a place in the managers' dining room. I roamed the company almost at will throughout Europe and Scandinavia and, for a time, cranked out a story a day. We fed these stories directly to the media in some export markets, and in countries in which Ford had PR managers, to the national PR departments for appropriate placement in their local media.

The European PR managers in particular were delighted. Most of them had no journalistic background and, although they worked hard and successfully at maintaining close contact with key media people, they needed written ammunition to exploit fully the sympathetic, friendly relations they were nurturing with the press. They had been going into battle with unloaded guns. Now, after the long, leisurely, and hugely expensive lunches that are a feature of automative PR, they could follow up with a large selection of good editorial material, much of it offered to appropriate publications for exclusive use within their circulation areas.

PICTURES WITH THE WORDS

The power of what I was producing was augmented enormously by having the support of a really great photographic department. Soon the Ford photographers also were enthused with assignments in which they were challenged to produce strong news and feature pictures.

Much of my material came from just wandering around the engineering research departments in England and Germany and chatting with the staff. I pursued leads that often at first seemed unlikely media material but frequently resulted in stories and pictures that "sold" to a wide range of publications all over the world.

It was good internal PR also, making people who were interviewed feel important in the context of the organization as a whole, especially when an individual or a department was featured in the press and there were clippings to show around.

FOCUS ON THE DETAIL ACHIEVEMENTS

I remember getting great coverage from some of the most unlikely sources. One was an engineer who had spent years working on car-door locks. It appeared at first to be one of the most boring jobs in the world and hardly the stuff of headlines, especially because the locks are components that the average motorist never even thinks about. They certainly don't have the glamour to figure in advertising or other promotional activities. But when a person who has focused so strongly on such a detail talks about the object of a large portion of his or her waking life, you can discover fascinating stuff.

In fact, at that time, a lot of technologically interesting things were happening to car locks, especially with new safety standards in the United States and Europe that ensured they would not burst open in accidents. Of course, every motor manufacturer in the world was working on much the same technology, but Ford was envisioned as a leader in this and some other apparently insignificant areas of vehicle development, because we pushed out stories and pictures on what we were doing while the others kept largely quiet.

This worked very well in the area of safety. Everybody was using crash dummies—those articulated human shapes that sit in cars that are driven into barriers to test seat belts and other safety features. We wrote about our crash dummies in a way that made them seem almost human. I remember one very simple and cheaply produced picture that scored all over the world.

In Cologne, we seated the crash dummies on upright chairs in a circle, with a very straight-faced German engineer in the middle, to get a really great picture combining humor and human interest.

NEW TWISTS ON OLD CORN

It was a twist on those corny static group photos, which we have all had to suffer through from schooldays on. This treatment, though, had novelty and inherent humor, with the caption pushing a newsy angle that sent it moving straight across editors' desks onto feature and even news pages in a score of countries.

That example demonstrates that your writer-at-large must have a sense of visual newsworthiness, so that he or she can identify the picture opportunities while wandering around looking for copy. It's almost worth the investment if the writer only comes up with picture ideas and writes captions for them.

LIES COME BACK TO HAUNT YOU

Having a writer-at-large also gives a company or other organization a lot of opportunities to generate positive media coverage by issuing fabricated stories. I'm not talking about lies—in this business, your PR falsehoods will usually keep coming back to haunt you—as the tobacco and liquor companies now are finding out. I mean stories fabricated to exploit some other news peg when you haven't got one of your own strong enough to hang a release on.

I did that once with Jackie Stewart during a slack period. We needed to get better coverage in general-interest magazines—especially women's magazines, which normally would not devote much, if any, space to motoring. Our research showed women taking increasingly important roles in car-buying decisions, but we weren't talking to them through their own media, in which the editors almost automatically junked anything originating from a motor company.

WHEN THERE'S NO NEWS, CREATE IT

We had no new product news—indeed, very little of anything to keep the media releases flowing. And the northern hemisphere was heading into the summer "silly season" of holiday months, during which editors seek material and PR copy stands a better chance of finding a home. (A similar situation exists around Christmas, New Year's Day, and other major holidays when, although the newspapers may be smaller because of less advertising, the amount of editorial material available tends to drop also. I have exploited this situation for several clients, preparing releases well in advance to hit this slack time. You can exploit the situation further by liaising with editors who need to get more pages into production earlier because their staff will be on holiday.)

My sole corporate task at Ford at that time was to generate stories about my company and its products. I had no other responsibilities, so it was not only easy to get away from my desk but obligatory that I get moving and start writing to fill the seasonal gap in our flow of media releases. So photographer Ken Shipton and I hopped a plane to Geneva where Jackie Stewart had cleared most of a day in the frenetic schedule of the world champion racing driver. We had arranged that his wife Helen and their kids—a very photogenic family—also would be on hand.

GET PICTURES THAT WORK

Jackie's palatial Swiss home, where I once attended a fascinating dinner party with his neighbor, actor Peter Ustinov, is a tremendous photographic location. Ken ignored the stunning view and the graceful lines of the old house, and got close to Jackie and Helen and their children as we rapidly shot a series of pictures that would work for our target media: photographs showing a "typical" family packing and preparing the car for a long holiday trip.

Jackie is a consummate publicist and also has had a long-term contractual relationship with Ford, so he needed no direction to position himself as he pointed to various parts of the car that should be checked for safety and comfort before departure. The famous blue oval logo featured prominently, but naturally, in most of the shots.

Setting the childproof locks on the rear doors, examining the radial tires and disc brakes for wear, ensuring that the multi-adjustable seat was correctly positioned, loading the capacious trunk, and setting the superb through-flow air conditioning emphasized the comfort, safety, and convenience features of the Ford. Of course, every other car manufacturer also had these features, but we were setting up an almost subliminal message that the best of the world's drivers would not dream of taking his precious family on a long holiday journey in anything but this car.

When Jackie rushed away to catch a plane, Ken and I spent another hour with Helen, interviewing her as a motoring mother and photographing her packing suitcases and showing the clothes that an attractive, fashion-conscious, practical woman would take with her on holiday.

For one day's work, plus about the same amount of time spent at the office writing the stories and processing the pictures, we generated valuable quality editorial coverage in many countries. Particularly significant, we got into women's magazines and into the women's sections of the newspapers with a Ford story, coverage we could not have achieved with conventional media releases.

HUNGRY JOURNALISTS WORK BEST

There are a lot of messages in these examples about the power of having a writer-at-large. He or she should be a journalist with imagination and the ability to spot stories and angle them to meet the needs of a variety of different types of publications or electronic media outlets. You may do best for the least expense with a local scribe with a stack of bills to pay who is really hungry and adopts a practical, no-nonsense approach to get the copy flowing.

You want a lot of simple, lively stories about your enterprise that the journalist knows a free lance could sell independently. In most cases, you don't want deep research and highly literate copy that takes days or weeks to produce. It makes sense, then, to pay your writer on a project basis—a certain amount for every story you accept, for every column inch his material secures for you, or a combination of both methods of payment in the form of a basic rate plus a bonus for editorial published.

The writer's approach should be that of a free lance working for the target media, not primarily for you—although he or she will, of course, build the right plugs into the copy and pictures.

BIG NAMES MAY NOT WORK

I would not use a big name writer or one who has been a senior staff member on a leading publication, although many managers tend to go after what is perceived to be top expertise and a prestigious name. That kind of writer is appropriate for certain situations, like a sponsored book or article in a corporate publication. For the general-purpose writer-at-large, though, you need a competent hack from a tough school. They seem to be getting harder to find these days, but they're still around, often working for local papers or free-lancing furiously on a variety of beats.

An active free lance with a family to feed must be doing most of the things you need right—he or she should be fast, efficient, and able to angle stories so that they sell. A wire-service reporter, particularly one who has covered a varied, busy beat, also has a good background for this PR application.

NO-FRILLS WRITING

The writing style should reflect a no-frills, down-to-earth newspaper approach. The classic inverted pyramid is the rule. An attention-grabbing headline, a strong pithy opening that answers the key *who, what, when, where,* and *how* questions, followed by punchy copy with short sentences and paragraphs liberally sprinkled with facts and direct quotes will work best. Make it as self-contained as possible as you go along, so that it can be trimmed easily from the bottom, paragraph by paragraph.

That often happens literally on the make-up table, where paragraphs are sliced out one by one with a knife until the text will fit into the hole assigned for it. In the many publications around the world that still use hot metal type, paragraph-lengths of type will be lifted out by the subeditor and compositor working together on "the stone". With electronic editing and page make up, the paragraphs are deleted with a key stroke—but the principles of the inverted pyramid and trimming a story from the bottom remain the same.

LOOK FOR THE ANGLES

Get your writer to angle the story—even if only by changing the introduction—to make it more immediately relevant to different types of publications. This is easy on a word processor and can work wonders for the hit rate.

With trade or special interest publications, always include in the introduction information that makes your release immediately relevant to them. I try to get the relevance into the first three words. When I publicized a type of paint surface treatment for

Jackie Stewart is a PR practitioner's dream—indeed, he knows the best photographic angles better than some of us who are in the business. Note here how a basically routine picture has been made more interesting by the low, close angle.

boats, planes and automobiles, I placed it in magazines covering each of those categories of interest. The introduction strongly stated for the boating magazines that this was a new treatment for boats; for aviation publications, for aircraft; and for the car magazines and motoring editors, for autos.

Let the copy run if it is strong enough—successful free lances, paid by the word, are adept at this and can turn a few words into a major news or feature piece that justifies its use at length, a very different technique from simply padding a story with uninteresting details. Make sure, though, that the story still can be cut easily from the bottom to fit it into the space available.

THE BENEFITS OF TIMELESSNESS

Try to make your releases as timeless as possible. The one about the Stewarts was used in different parts of the world as a holiday-season feature for a full year and kept on cropping up in unexpected places for a long time afterwards. I heard that a number of editors liked the theme and the bundle of pictures so much that they pushed the package into a drawer and just waited for the right opportunity to publish.

That element of timelessness was enhanced by close-ups. Changes in car styling can date a picture very quickly, but we focused tightly on details that are not readily distinguishable from one year's model to the next. Of course, the Ford and other companies' logos seem to exist forever, although you should be careful if a logo change by your company or client is in the offing.

Also, by not making visual or written material time-sensitive, you can use the material internationally more easily. A product with a distinctive appearance may have a far longer life in overseas markets than it does in the trend-conscious United States or European territories, so overseas subsidiaries may still be running with a version of a product that has been superseded in the source countries.

Additionally, trends themselves may take a long time to travel around the world. What happens in California today may still make news in Europe, Africa, or other parts of the world a year hence.

HANDLING THE PICTURES

Unless it really is impossible, always send out all editorial material with visuals. High-contrast, glossy, black-and-white photographs are suitable for most publications, but shoot the same subjects on color transparency film at the same time and make it clear in the release and the captions that color is available. Good color pictures can be offered exclusively to key publications, while your general distribution uses black-and-whites.

I prefer, if circumstances permit, to get the photographer to shoot a lot of similar color shots on-the-spot, rather than relying completely on duplicating his or her best efforts later. This often can be the most economical way of building up an immediate stock of "original dupes". Slight changes in angle and content also give you more variety to offer to editors.

Thirty-five-millimeter transparencies are now almost universally acceptable to editors, because lenses and film stock have been developed to the point where these small images will blow up without losing too much quality. However, for a really great picture, especially one aimed at being used as a front cover, the large 2¼ square negative format is preferable. It looks more impressive when it arrives on the editor's desk, is easier to preview, and will reproduce better.

Your writer-at-large may also be a competent photographer, but that's a hard combination to find. When hiring a photographer, look for attributes similar to those you want in the writer. I've had considerable success using young (but competent) enthusiastic amateur photographers who are trying to break into the professional market. They do not have the expertise and experience of the professional you would use for specific advertising or annual-report photography, but the right choice should produce the kind of pictures that work editorially.

DON'T BE *TOO* CREATIVE

The pictures for this kind of publicity need to meet accepted press standards. Good contrast, not too much cluttering detail, strong subject matter and a novel angle all contribute to acceptance. Remember that, even in this day and age, many local and small-circulation publications still reproduce halftones fairly badly. An over-creative photographer trying to achieve subtleties of tone and composition may actually decrease your scoring rate.

One editor I know uses only line drawings, because he will not accept the poor quality of half-tone reproduction that his printer and paper permit. (Incidentally, he still gets bombarded with publicity halftones from PR people who have never bothered to study his publication and refine their mailing lists according to his needs.)

Always get human interest in the picture, as demonstrated in this shot, which was used to illustrate the technical story on robotics discussed earlier. Cover the two figures on the left with your hand and see how their absence detracts from the appeal of the picture.

This illustration benefits from having the equipment being handled by someone and shot from an interesting angle. The white coat adds a sense of authority and provides a light background, which makes the hardware stand out better. A white coat also gives you an excuse to get the corporate logo well into the picture without seeming obtrusive. Carry a selection of logos with you and fasten them in place with double-sided tape or similar adhesives.

HUMAN INTEREST WORKS

Always get human interest in the picture. Only in the technical journals did I get much use out of detailed product pictures (e.g., for the car door locks). There was a much better hit rate for pictures of the engineer quoted in the story *doing* something related to locks, such as examining one that had survived a crash test.

If there is a manager or executive featured in the story who cannot logically be doing something physically related to a product, then at least get him or her away from the desk and in a visually interesting situation. Straight head-and-shoulders shots are a last resort.

There may be problems in overcoming executives' often misguided protection of their own perceived self-image, so you need tact and a proper explanation if the subjects suspect they will look foolish. Some even resist being pictured out of business suits, and I've had problems with engineers and researchers who generally work in white coats but who have wanted to be photographed in their laboratories or testing facilities wearing totally inappropriate formal suits and ties to avoid being mistaken for subordinate technicians.

The Germans and French, I have found, tend to be the most difficult in this respect. One German engineer made an international call to check on my rank in the corporate hierarchy before he would cooperate with my photographer and me and was so wooden and conservative in his attitude that we just couldn't get good pictures of him.

The corporate or product identification in a picture must be natural and unobtrusive in nearly all cases. Otherwise, any self-respecting editor won't use it. The exceptions are some business and trade publications, in which the company or product identification is important in its own right to readers.

Getting a logo in a shot—in focus!—may be enough. When I was a writer-at-large, I used to carry in my briefcase a selection of logos, badges, and so on, with double-sided tape or that wonderful stuff you can get in some countries that looks and feels like putty. When you knead it, there is a chemical reaction that makes it temporarily adhesive. With these aids, you can quickly and temporarily fasten a logo to clothing, a product, or equipment in a manufacturing plant or laboratory in the most appropriate place for photography.

BEWARE OF THE BACKGROUND

Always examine the background, especially in factories or plants in which there may be something—like a pile of garbage, a scruffy sign, or a new piece of machinery that the competition should not know about—that must not be in the picture. I once set up a shot by a main road outside a client's plant, and a truck advertising his main rival's products passed by in the background without anyone realizing it until we printed the negatives. We had to go back and do the photo shoot all over again, with egg on our faces.

Exploit the location whenever you can. I was promoting a movie called *Silver Bears,* starring the very tall actor Bo Svenson, and needed pictures for a story featuring him and the marketing boss of the film's local distribution company. The only place I could get them together was a Los Angeles gym where Bo was working out. I quickly set up a shot of the executive reaching up to touch the top of Bo's head as the actor stood there in a sweaty T-shirt against a background of weightlifting equipment.

A caption had to give some kind of rationale for this rather bizarre posing, so we turned that picture into a whole promotional program. We ran a competition through a cooperating newspaper for readers to estimate Bo's height. The prize was a weekend in a hotel that claimed to cater to any individual whim or need—including a suite with a giant bed for those of Bo Svenson dimensions. The competition cost virtually nothing, but achieved a greater response than a very expensive promotion for a much bigger movie that offered really valuable prizes.

BOAST IN THE TRADES

Never hesitate to brag through your trade press about your PR successes. We gave the details of this promotion to a movie industry monthly. The marketing executive was delighted to be included in his trade magazine and got much favorable comment from his colleagues, although he had been nervous about posing for a picture that he feared might make him look rather silly. Don't embarrass anyone in your PR efforts—especially not the boss or the client!

A good writer- or photographer-at-large will identify such opportunities for pictures about your publicity efforts, and they can be a valuable spin-off from the main task of producing the more standard editorial material.

A DIFFERENT PERSPECTIVE

At the start of this section, I recommended against using a staff member as the writer, mainly for the practical reason of time. But the different attitude and perspective of an outside free lance are important also.

A creative, curious outsider may identify things about your organization and its people that a staffer, close to the action, does not perceive as being of wider interest. Even a free lance can become part of the organization quite quickly and lose his or her detached objectivity, so if output in quantity and quality starts to decline, consider bringing in someone with a fresh perspective.

I found it increasingly difficult as a writer-at-large with Ford to maintain the perspective of a curious outsider given *carte blanche* to probe the mysteries of a giant corporation. Too soon I started to become a company man, and then I really died as a fully effective writer when the manager I was reporting to landed the job of PR director for a rival manufacturer.

When he resigned, the security people supervised him as he cleared out his desk and left the building. They do this in large, security-conscious organizations when a key employee goes to a rival, in case he or she plans to take any confidential documents. It's often equivalent to locking the corporate stable door after the horse has escaped. I moved up to his position and immediately got involved in memo-writing, staffing matters, and endless committee meetings that made producing creative editorial material a seemingly lower priority task—so it rarely got done.

PROTECT YOUR WRITER

Nurture and protect your writer-at-large from such distractions. If your operation is not big enough to employ a full-time writer, use the benefits of this facility by employing a part-time free lance. Unfortunately, you may not get such a service easily and economically through your PR agency, so it may be worth recruiting the writer yourself and getting the agency to process and place the material.

Whatever the tactics, do think carefully about getting an investigative, creative, and productive writer and photographer involved with your organization. If they are good, they will produce a mass of material you never suspected was lurking there. Virtually all of it can be used in internal publications (e.g., an employee newspaper), and a very high proportion should find homes in external media, where it can contribute mightily to your marketing communications needs.

WRITING BY COMMITTEE DOESN'T WORK

The writer-at-large concept can be used also to resolve the many problems that arise when executives—particularly in collaboration—try to produce a written communication intended for either internal or external audiences.

Ruth G. Norman, an independent business communications consultant, highlighted the problems in an excellent piece in *Personnel Journal,* in which she said, "Too often, after spending time and energy discussing strategies, those responsible for the final document are haphazard about allocating writing responsibilities. Creating a systematic, collaborative process that is fine tuned to take into account each contributor's talents, time constraints, normal job responsibility, rank in the organization and commitment to the project is essential."

Collaborative business writing usually fails to communicate. The results are almost invariably too long and convoluted, reflecting the efforts of each author to protect his or her area of interest.

The truth is that committees or groups just cannot produce good writing. Shakespeare's works could not have been produced by a committee, and Thomas Jefferson was forced to write the Declaration of Independence on his own in order to bring a consensus of views into a crisp, high-impact, and literate document. The Bible is one of the few examples of group writing that works, and I suspect that even in that case some of the original authors would not be too pleased with the outcome.

One of the big friction points in the news magazines and some newspapers is the way that reporters and correspondents feel that their copy is mauled by writers, editors, and other desk workers. It was a constant complaint of mine when I was covering the Biafra war for *Newsweek* that the meaning of my original drafts could be changed during the convoluted editing process—and no organization gets even close to the editing skills that the leading news magazines deploy.

COMBATTING INFLATED EGOS

Even if a business communication is assigned to a skilled editor for final writing, that editing task is inevitably compromised by the pressures—real or imagined—exerted by the original authors. When a group of vice-presidents sit down to hammer out a corporate mission statement, there is a power struggle to get individual views and senses of importance across. Couple those motivations with contrasting styles—from the conversationally informal to the detailed, long, and convoluted writing of so many businesspeople—and you get a draft that is a communications mess.

An editor cannot merely tidy up such a document, which Ruth Norman compares with "a portrait painted jointly by Andrew Wyeth and Andy Warhol". It usually demands a complete rewrite, which predictably sets off a lot of arguments and further revisions.

You get rid of all that nonsense if the CEO appoints a professional writer who gathers information from all the relevant people and then goes away to do a proper communications job to present those views and facts in a concise, clear and motivating way. Obviously it is wise to give senior executives, line managers and any other relevant staff the opportunity to respond to the document, but final approval must lie with one person, preferably the CEO.

IMMUNITY TO PEER PRESSURE

Even when an organization has a competent professional writer on staff, it may be expedient to go outside to a free lance to get an important written statement prepared. Such an outsider should be more immune to internal peer and other pressures than an insider and better able to defend his or her writing from the point of view of its qualities in effectively communicating to the target audience.

When Is a Ghost Immoral?
Ethical problems in PR

The Larry Speakes Affair has caused a lot of soul-searching in PR circles—and much moralistic nonsense about the ethics of PR people putting words into their clients' mouths.

For years, some of the most effective PR I have ever done was for two CEOs who allowed me to get close enough to both them as individuals and to their businesses so that I routinely drafted speeches, media releases, letters, and statements attributable to them without ever sitting down and discussing them beforehand. The bond of understanding and the trust between us was such that sometimes those statements would go out unchecked by the CEOs concerned. I was never happy about that, but time pressures and other logistical problems occasionally made it seem expedient.

This kind of thing goes on all the time in industry and politics. Conversations between PR and media people about an issue on which the PR person's organization has adopted a viewpoint often end with the question from the journalist, "Who can I attribute that to?" The answer frequently is, "It's OK to say that comes from the Chairman", and so another direct quote from an authoritative figure gets into print without the journalist and the source ever having been in direct contact.

Since Larry Speakes published his kiss-and-tell book about his work as President Reagan's spokesman, this practice of concocting quotes has been called seriously into question from an ethical viewpoint. Speakes resigned from his $250,000 job as spokesman for Merrill Lynch & Company and got a blasting from all quarters.

"Public relations did not need Speakes' irresponsible actions," wrote Ron Rogers, president of the Los Angeles PR firm Rogers & Associates, in the *Los Angeles Times*. (Rogers noted that he did not have time to write the article himself, but went over each point with one of his staff and approved the tone and content.)

"Nor has the industry needed the embarrassment brought by those public relations people who have knowingly issued inaccurate or misleading information on behalf of national leaders, corporate chieftains, and celebrities."

LET'S BE REALISTIC

No one could argue with that comment, nor with the emphasis
Rogers placed on the approval process before statements are issued. However, we must be realistic and put some of the blame—if
there is blame—on the hungry media who much prefer to quote authoritative, *real* sources rather than mere spokespeople. Rogers says
that "public relations people should set high standards and ethics for
themselves, and not allow themselves to be bullied by press who
want a real source."

We got around the problem at Ford by being well-briefed on key
matters and then speaking not just as spokespeople but as individuals
with positions of authority in the company. Permission was given for
individuals to be quoted by name and title quite a long way down
the hierarchy if their responsibilities made them the appropriate
source for a particular topic (e.g., an engineer specializing in braking
components, if that was the subject of the story).

Rules about spokespeople that combine practicality with reasonable ethical standards should be written down and observed in
any organization. If a responsible PR person is sufficiently close to,
say, the CEO, then he or she could prepare and issue statements attributable to the CEO; in this case, there should be a clear understanding that the CEO will back them. Except in extreme situations,
those statements should always be cleared by the person to whom
they are attributed.

It can get ridiculous if carried to extremes. I had a CEO client
who always felt very uneasy dealing with the media and allowed
me too much rope to do so in his name. I had to curtail the practice
when he didn't read the drafts or reports I sent him, especially when
journalists got through to him to follow up stories in which he was
quoted, and he had to ask them to read back what he was purported
to have said!

DELEGATING RESPONSIBILITY

That experience presented me with the kind of ethical problems
about ghosting that many PR people face. It is a reality of modern
life that the bosses have to delegate a whole range of functions

that are executed in their name, from check signing to ensuring the integrity of a firm's products and services. It seems reasonable, then, to delegate the issuing of statements from a company figurehead to a responsible colleague who is close to the source and who fully understands the tone and content that the source would use if it was practical for him or her to speak directly to the media all the time.

However, I would always prefer that the responsibility for issuing organizational statements and comments is delegated along with other functional responsibilities, and that those to whom the responsibility is delegated may be quoted directly in their own name. It is inhibiting to good, constructive PR if only the head of an organization can converse openly and attributably with the media.

A SIGN OF MATURITY

I think an organization has matured from the viewpoints of PR and its own culture if media people can talk with the most appropriate staff member and then be free to quote that staff member directly by name and title without prior approval.

Then the PR people can fulfill a liaison role, facilitating the contact and standing back to let the source and the media communicate directly without inhibition or the risk of ethical conflict. Such a policy represents an open organization with little to conceal and no fear of being misinterpreted, apart from the obvious unavoidable risk of comments being misquoted or used out of context.

You cannot perform really good PR for a firm that does not have such an open policy and does not trust its people to speak responsibly and accurately about its affairs. Such an organization rarely has the need to contrive quotes, because it has a number of authoritative spokespeople who can be named in the attribution. But we need the media to cooperate, to accept and use such quotes, and to not be so insistent on tagging a celebrity name on their stories.

Section 2

It Doesn't Pay to Cheat

How an advertising agency tried too hard to get new business and inspired PR turned an embarrassment into a corporate image coup

Few professional business services present more temptations for cheating than publicity and promotional activities. Yet you deceive at your peril, for the consequences of being found out can be horrible.

The one exception to that rule is the entertainment business, particularly the movies. The truth is a subjective concept in "fantasyland" PR. Ever since the industry began, press agents have lied and the media have happily peddled those untruths, as long as they make good copy. It's all part of an elaborate game.

In more conventional business activities, it pays to be honest, truthful, and ethical. Rob Lebow, when he was the Director of Corporate Communications for Microsoft Inc., the world's biggest computer software supplier, proved the point in the classic case that set the advertising and computer industries buzzing from coast to coast.

Microsoft's main advertising account was up for grabs, and more than a score of leading agencies were scrambling to pitch for $15 million per year in billings.

An east coast advertising agency sent to Lebow a mail shot which will become a classic in the perennial debate about the extent to which agencies can be aggressive and risk compromising ethical standards when competing for new business.

THE BIG TEMPTATION

Inside the envelope to Lebow was a round-trip airline ticket and an invitation to learn about the inside marketing plans of Microsoft's arch rival, Lotus Development Corp. It came at a crucial stage in the clash of these two software titans, with Lotus preparing an offensive to protect its 1-2-3 spreadsheet program against the launch of Microsoft's hot new PC Excel. It was rather like Wellington being offered a briefing on Napoleon's planned strategy for Waterloo.

"Since we know your competition's plans, isn't it worth taking a flier?" the agency asked Lebow.

"You see, the reason we know so much about Lotus is that some of our newest employees just spent the past year and a half working on the Lotus business at another agency. So they are intimately acquainted with Lotus' thoughts about Microsoft—and their plans to deal with the introduction of Excel".

It was cute copy and an imaginative pitch, but somebody at the agency really goofed in not following one of the golden rules in the communication business—research your audience. Lebow is meticulous in everything, particularly corporate ethics, on which he speaks frequently. He immediately rejected the approach and turned it round into a *cause celebre* with many positive benefits for Microsoft's image.

He sent back the invitation—and the ticket—with a curt note informing the agency that they had totally eliminated themselves from consideration. That same day Microsoft passed all the facts on to Lotus, who got a court order restraining the agency from divulging any Lotus trade secrets. For the record, the agency denied any attempt at industrial espionage and maintained it was only offering "related experience" from two new associate creative directors hired the previous month from Lotus's main agency.

TRUST IS A PRICELESS ASSET

A reputation for being trustworthy is a priceless asset in any industry—computers in particular. Software developers, like Microsoft and Lotus, need to know the advanced plans of hardware manufacturers, such as Apple and IBM, because their products are interdependent. As a result of Rob Lebow's response in the agency incident, Microsoft demonstrated in a dramatic way that it can be trusted, even in extreme situations of competition and possible temptation. The company's corporate image was enhanced both within its own industry and in the marketplace generally, with valuable media coverage that the company never could have bought. The editorial exposure in the *Wall Street Journal* alone was worth many thousands of dollars.

The case is important to all PR and advertising professionals because of the reaction it has generated among the business community. Agency people often fail to realize just how concerned many clients are about their confidential information being revealed to competitors. This concern goes much deeper than just the leaking of marketing campaigns or new product information.

THE CONFIDENTIAL CONNECTION

The PR and advertising account executives involved in client contact functions often become very close to key client executives in both the personal and the corporate sense. As a result, they may have more opportunities than anyone outside the client company to acquire intelligence that could be useful to a rival.

Their roles as communications consultants often extend into the client company's most sensitive areas and it is accepted that close personal relationships will be forged, both socially and in the workplace. Often the PR or advertising professional is with the client's senior executives when they are at their most vulnerable, for example, when away from the disciplines of base and under stress, such as at sales conventions, exhibitions, dealer meetings, and so on.

Many account executives have found themselves acting as soulmates for clients who have had too much to drink or want a sympathetic ear into which to unload corporate—even domestic—frustrations.

If the client is not as rigidly scrupulous about corporate ethics as Lebow and Microsoft, a PR or advertising consultant takes a big risk even by being sympathetic to a client's temptation to pull a questionable stunt or bend the truth in a media release. Even basically dishonest clients may feel more comfortable with honest advisers.

PR ABUSE TO GENERATE TRUST

I had personal experience of this while handling a PR account for an entertainment industry company with an executive who was justifiably regarded with great suspicion, even in that inherently dishonest business. He chose well-regarded professionals to be his PR consultant and most visible lawyer and accountant.

Of course, he was using our reputations to enhance his own image and we all resigned his very lucrative business when we found ourselves being tarnished by the association, even if we were not being put into situations in which we risked compromising our own principles.

No, you really cannot afford *not* to be ethical and honest in the PR business. Cheating doesn't pay, but playing the white knight, as Lebow demonstrated, can be highly cost-effective.

Honesty Pays with a Fake Photo
You don't need big budgets to make a large impact

One of the big problems for PR people working on accounts related to motor racing is that the general-interest media are really only interested in action pictures of disaster. The motoring magazines may carry shots of your horrendously expensive 200 m.p.h. mobile billboards going around the circuit, but the general media are really only interested when the cars crash or are on fire, with consequent nasty negative imagery for your client.

Another problem in exploiting visual opportunities from sporting events is that they are so time critical. If there is a good picture, you must get it out fast, and often the logistics and the cost of doing so present many difficulties.

We had such a problem at Ford when the company's sponsored Grand Prix engine was due to score its milestone 100th win at the Watkins Glen circuit in the United States. Ford's involvement in Grand Prix racing was the cornerstone of a multimillion dollar international campaign to change the company's image from a manufacturer of rather boring, plainly engineered cars to the supplier of the more exotic, sporty transport the market was demanding in the seventies.

POWERFUL AND IN GOOD TIME

We needed a powerful picture marking that 100th win to send to a wide range of publications around the world in every country in which Ford was active. The various time zones and deadlines made that logistically impossible if we were to rely on a shot from the event itself—and, anyway, a shot of another racing car passing a checkered flag would have obtained very limited exposure in the general media, and our engine or logo would not even have been visible.

Budget was no real problem, so I made an attempt to see if we could get 100 racing cars together to create a dramatic picture, but it

This picture generated enormous media coverage and overcame a number of problems in a very practical way. When the Ford Formula One engine was due to notch up its 100th victory at Watkins Glen, I needed a very special photograph to publicize this fact. A major handicap was the difference in time zones between North America and my other international markets and the need to create a photograph for long-lead publications that could be distributed well ahead of the motor-racing milestone.

So I borrowed 100 diecast toy models of racing cars using the Ford engine and took them to the famous Brands Hatch grand prix circuit near London. Photographer Ken Denyer and I created a unique picture of 100 cars on the grid symbolizing the 100 victories. We distributed black-and-white prints and color transparencies around the world and generated far greater coverage than we would have received for a conventional shot of the actual event. The picture went beyond being just a visual from a motorsport event and so got used on news and feature pages as well—even magazine front covers.

Here is how Ken Denyer took the shot, an interesting picture in its own right that gave me a chance to get some actual product exposure as well by including a production car in the background for scale. This "picture-behind-the-picture" earned extensive editorial coverage also. Both shots were used in a news feature in the mass circulation *London Daily Express;* that alone more than merited the not very great effort we put into this PR project.

was impossible. My solution emerged over lunch with an executive of the Corgi toy company, which specializes in beautifully detailed diecast scale models of vehicles, including Grand Prix racers. They loaned me 100 models of Grand Prix cars that used the Ford engine, painted in the different liveries of the teams.

Then I got into a huddle with Ford's veteran staff photographer, Ken Denyer. Although only recently back at work after a very serious operation, Ken displayed real enthusiasm for the project and demonstrated that, while the PR consultant may have the spark of an idea, it can take professional artistic, photographic, or other talent to turn it into reality.

Ken set those 100 models out on the actual tarmac in front of the stands at one of Europe's leading Grand Prix circuits near London. Then, with a long focus lens, he took a shot that played clever tricks with the perspective to make the tiny toys look like real racers revving up on the starting grid.

HONESTY PAYS

The picture was so realistic that I was tempted to encourage editors to use it to fool their readers, making it appear a genuine motor racing shot with the deception only revealed in the accompanying caption. But we actually increased our coverage by emphasizing that it was a staged shot and revealing all the technical details up front.

I distributed another picture that showed Ken down on the tarmac with his camera in front of the models. The accompanying caption contained technical information about the lens, film, and exposures used. This shot was the only way we could get acceptable product exposure (we used a Ford production car as a scale comparison). The picture revealing how we took the main shot was actually more valuable to the company in sales-related publicity and lots of publications used it.

We shot both pictures in black-and-white and color transparencies. The Ford of Europe photographic laboratories under Steve Clark produced hundreds of superb prints and duplicate slides.

The final links in the chain of this successful media publicity effort were Ford's very talented international team of national PR managers. I sent them the pictures and accompanying story, together with background features and a complete press kit on Ford's engineering activities in motorsport around the world. The PR managers and their staffs in each of the sales territories then distributed this material, in many cases at special meetings with key editors to offer territorial exclusivity.

Even before the Watkins Glen Grand Prix started, our pictures and story were in type and ready to run by many publications. Because the Ford engine dominated Formula One racing at the time, a win was virtually certain. The exposure that single picture got—including magazine front covers in full color—was enormous, probably the most cost-effective PR stunt I have ever undertaken.

Yet, like all the best ideas, it was basically simple and inexpensive. Also, like the best publicity projects, it was successful because of the professionalism and team work of the people involved.

Section 3

The Write Stuff

*How Parker Pen achieved the ultimate
in product endorsement and etched its
place in history before the ink dried*

Celebrity product endorsement causes PR and advertising people many headaches. Often clients are beguiled into sponsorships and other deals because of their own personal interests, and the PR person then has to make the venture cost-effective. That happens a lot when corporations sponsor golf games and other sports events played by executives or make donations to favored charities.

I remember working once with a bank and a motor manufacturer who were joint sponsors of an international squash tournament. Squash is a minority interest sport that is similar to racquetball and is played inside a concrete box, which severely limits both the number of spectators who can view it and decent camera angles for both still and television pictures.

In sheer desperation, when world champion Geoff Hunt won the tournament, I had his cheque painted on the hood of one sponsor's car and Geoff drove it into the other sponsor's bank to get it cashed. We got better photographic coverage for that than the entire tournament had provided, with good product exposure for my two clients. But it was a terribly contrived stunt that could not be repeated frequently.

SIGNING HISTORY

The Parker Pen Company had much more going for it when President Ronald Reagan and Soviet leader Mikhael Gorbachev used its products to sign the historic agreement eliminating intermediate-range nuclear weapons. This was a perfectly executed exploitation with professional followup that lasted until Parker received the ultimate accolade of media coverage about how clever the PR effort had been.

President Reagan often signed documents with felt tip pens—well, he would, wouldn't he? A smart Parker sales representative on the State Department account acted to move the signing tools upmarket the moment he heard of the planned summit. Before rivals Sheaffer or Cross could react, special $250 sterling silver versions of Parker's fountain pens were made for the historic signing by the two leaders—effectively a product endorsement by the two most powerful men on earth.

It took only six weeks to organize, but this publicity coup will keep paying off for Parker for years to come. The company is still getting mileage out of the facts that Puccini wrote *La Boheme* with a Parker and that the Parker pens of Dwight Eisenhower were used to sign the treaty at the end of World War II in Europe.

SLICK FOLLOWUP

The followup for the Reagan-Gorbachev exposure was as slick and professional as the planning. Parker spent a half-million dollars on full-page advertisements showing the signing. The copyline was, "The pen is mightier than the sword. The historic document is signed. The pen is a Parker". Parker's media-relations people made sure the message was picked up editorially and will continue working to exploit the long-term benefits of their product's link with history.

A problem with special one-shot, celebrity-exposure examples of a product is that the VIP usually keeps it; then you have nothing to display for more publicity. Duplicates can be very useful. Gorbachev and Reagan kept their pens, but Parker made an identical back-up pair, in case the others failed to work.

Surprisingly, they did not exploit the obvious opportunity to produce a "limited edition" replica run of the summit pen, which should have sold like hot cakes.

"Parkers have been used by U.S. Presidents since the Truman Administration. Offering replicas of this one may have been perceived as distasteful by both the public and the administration," commented Gene Rohlman, Manager of Communications.

Marketing Hype for Lazer Gun-Slingers

Sharp-shooting promotions can build up enormous prelaunch demand, but your credibility will be shot down if you can't deliver on your promises

Far too often, the marketing people don't talk enough with their production colleagues. Even the most imaginative promotional campaigns can leave the whole company with egg on its face if the demand generated by publicity is not matched to the capacity to deliver the goods.

That happens a lot in the book publishing, computer software and consumer electronics industries, when the media give exposure to a hot new title or product but the stores are not stocked to turn the exposure into sales. Every year one or more toy manufacturers get caught out by imbalances in supply and demand.

Worlds of Wonder, Inc. experienced that. The young California toy company had taken off like a rocket with the success of its talking teddy bear. The garrulous teddy was followed by a high tech Lazer Tag game, which beat major competitors to the marketplace with a new generation of chase and catch toys using infrared beams.

STRONG PRELAUNCH DEMAND

A $7 million advertising and promotional budget behind Lazer Tag ran like clockwork, building up strong prelaunch demand. It opened with carefully targeted teaser ads on cable television, then high-level exposure—to generate both media and word-of-mouth coverage—in the form of a celebrity Lazer Tag competition at a Hollywood nightclub. Get well-known people having fun with any product and you are guaranteed a host of good photographic opportunities.

A Saturday morning animated cartoon television show clicked in right on schedule to expose the kids to the product. The potential market was broadened by a series of college Lazer Tag tournaments designed to generate awareness among this difficult-to-reach young adult sector.

As a result, the Lazer Tag brand name became the generic description for a whole new product category—the Xerox of this sector of the toy business. The PR, promotions, and advertising made Lazer Tag the instinctive consumer first choice when buying high-tech tag games. Sadly, the marketing hype was out of sync with supply capacity.

Worlds of Wonder's image suffered because it was unable to deliver sufficient quantities to catch the peak Christmas selling season demand. That compounded retailers' already negative feelings about the company because of technical problems many had experienced with the talking bear.

Worlds of Wonder demonstrated, particularly with its college tournament promotion, that imaginative toy marketing can be very cost-effective. It showed also that constant monitoring and interpretation of market reaction, together with accurate predictions of demand, are essential if the publicity is not going to take off and leave the product grounded because motivated customers cannot buy.

Sports Celebrities Can Be an Expensive Nuisance

How a shy Czech tennis phenomenon came through for Avis and Adidas

Millions of sports sponsorship dollars are wasted by companies that do not take a long-term attitude or fail to establish good working relationships with the star performers they have under contract. Notable exceptions are Adidas and Avis, the car rental firm, because of the way they have handled their long association with the consistently successful tennis player, Ivan Lendl.

The two corporations got into one of the hottest sponsorship deals in world tennis as a result of having advisers with tennis expertise, who could evaluate Lendl's potential. Securing a relationship with a sports star on his way up can save a company vast amounts of money and also help to build a relationship that ensures the kind of positive, cooperative attitude by the star that cannot be boiled down into black and white in a contract.

A SPONSORSHIP GAMBLE

Lendl's tennis-playing potential was clear, but he must have represented a gamble for his sponsors because his looks and nature were negative elements from a marketing viewpoint. The inherently shy Czech emigré spoke very little English at first, while his stern facial features made him appear cold and hostile. That Lendl scowl is projected particularly strongly when the cameras zoom in on him as he concentrates at crucial points in a game—just at the moment when the Adidas and Avis patches on his shirt also come into focus!

But the two corporations—and Proserv, Inc., the sports marketing company that represented Lendl—have gained a far more powerful PR vehicle as Lendl has worked with them to change his image and make his enormous fees far more cost-effective. He now pulls in over $6 million a year from endorsements and exhibition matches, so the public transformation of Ivan Lendl has been a PR program of great financial significance to himself as well as to his sponsors.

In a carefully planned series of interviews and personal appearances, Lendl's public image has been enhanced and now comes across more in keeping with his real personality. He still glares just as coldly at his opponent—and at the cameras—when he is concentrating on court, but that is far more acceptable now to consumers who have been exposed to positive, "nice-guy" information about a Lendl who loves dogs and children, does a lot of charity work, and even makes a real effort to be nice to journalists.

INTERNAL PR ALSO

Avis and Adidas also find the more mature, affable, and self-confident Lendl much more useful in a wide range of close-contact and internal PR situations. He gave Avis staff morale a tremendous boost on a visit to the company's headquarters and is friendly and enthusiastic when being used to impress important clients at cocktail parties and other social engagements.

The experience with Lendl proves several key points about PR and sports celebrities. Much of the PR effort will be wasted unless the star is basically a nice guy (or gal, like that darling of the sponsors, Chrissie Evert). If Lendl really were the arrogant, cold character that his initial public image projected, then he could be counter-productive in lots of PR situations.

CATER TO IDIOSYNCRACIES

It is always necessary for the corporate people to make a positive effort to motivate and cater to the inevitable idiosyncrasies of even the most cooperative star. Adidas and Avis have worked with Lendl to make the most of their business association during their long-running relationship with him. He now understands the promotional needs of both companies and is motivated to pursue their interests.

The payback—for both Lendl and his sponsors—will continue over an extended period of time as his contract enables their relationship to mature. As Lendl fades out of competitive tennis, he plans, as other sportsmen have done, to become more active in corporate promotional work.

Comparatively few companies appreciate the value of providing for a long-term relationship that extends way beyond a sporting star's peak. One of the classic examples of how effective such a relationship can be is the way that Ford and former world champion racing driver Jackie Stewart have continued their association for many years. It became second nature for Jackie subtly to plug Ford's interests from formal media receptions to occasions such as the party in Austria where journalists joined him in racing model slot-cars.

However successful a star may be in his or her heyday, he or she fears what will happen when an inevitably short career is over, and the spotlight—and the big money—move on to the next generation. A star will make a greater effort for a corporate sponsor who forges meaningful long-term relationships that go beyond the specified fine print of the contract.

If You Haven't Got an Angle—Write a Book

How Pepsi's former boss demonstrated that a business book can be an ideal peg on which to hang a PR program and sweeten a sour Apple

An important trend in business book publishing is to use a biography or corporate story as a strong peg on which to hang a PR campaign. In some respects it is a dangerous trend. The PR benefits can be so enourmous that there will be increasing temptation for books to be released and promoted as genuine examples of literature, when in fact they are primarily tools of a marketing program far removed from the true business of publishing.

John Sculley's book about his career with Pepsi and Apple Computers is a good read and so a legitimate publishing venture. But it has probably done as much for Apple Computer's business as Lee Iaccocca's phenomenal best-seller did for Chrysler's image.

REVIEWS ARE VALUABLE

Even if nobody bought Sculley's book, the reviews and published extracts alone have proved immensely valuable to Apple. This exposure, made possible because of the existence of the book, has done much to restore Apple's image after the departure of Steve Jobs and has boosted market awareness of several new product lines. Let us look at just two of many examples.

The magazine *Personal Computing* ran long excerpts over several pages with powerful color visuals, and the *Los Angeles Times* is typical of the many newspapers and magazines which picked up various aspects of the book to support extensive—and repeated—news and feature coverage.

HITTING THE PRIME TARGETS

In December 1987, *Personal Computing* was hitting Apple's prime target market with pages of Sculley's inside information about Jobs's resignation that would fascinate both computer buffs and the general business book reader. The way it came across reinforced both Sculley's position as CEO and Apple's corporate image as a strong, ethical, and progressive company that could actually benefit from the departure of one its famous founders.

While that excerpt was on the bookshelves, Lawrence J. Magid's widely read "Computer File" column in the *Los Angeles Times* tackled a completely different aspect of Sculley's book. Magid built a very readable column around the book's deliberately vague references to future technology on which Apple is working.

USING FANTASY PRODUCTS

The futuristic product called "Knowledge Navigator", which Sculley discusses in his book and in countless interviews, may prove to have about as much substance as the advanced-concept cars that auto manufacturers wheel out at shows when they haven't got any exciting new product to publicize. Nevertheless, it has generated a lot of very positive corporate exposure for Apple with the specific benefit of reassuring its market that the company is here to stay for a long time and will continue to be a technological innovator. These are vital image factors in maintaining consumer confidence in the computer business. Maintaining media exposure in the intervals between major corporate events or new product announcements can be extremely difficult, but Apple's publicists have demonstrated effectively how a book provides a very acceptable topical peg.

If the publicists are involved in a corporate book project early, they can greatly influence its benefits to the company and products. Also, they can extend the working life of the publicity peg by structuring a campaign that will highlight certain key elements of the book at different times to different target audiences.

The author needs to be strong on exploitation to realize the potential of his book. Sculley is a competent PR performer who proved adept at steering radio and television interviewers away from the strong human interest aspect of his book—the split with Jobs—to create opportunities for him to plug his company and its new generation of products.

BOARDROOM DRAMA

Another important PR element of the Sculley book is that it is strong in boardroom drama and consequently has broad appeal to business readers. Its release was timed to coincide with the movement by Apple into the growth market for business computers. The book—and the way it has been exploited—have made potential business users aware of Apple's Macintosh hardware in a highly cost-effective way. It has played a major role in transforming Apple's image from the supplier of easy-to-use home computers to a major producer of serious business computing applications. It is a model example of well-integrated marketing communications.

Observers of the PR scene will continue to find much of interest as Sculley's career develops and his personality benefits his company's corporate image. For example, his decision to take a sabbatical was very cleverly handled, generating extensive positive media coverage that reflected well on Apple's image as an employer.

Books are a powerful medium for publicity in many forms, because the publication of a bound volume can be turned into an exploitable *event* of considerable substance or used to commemorate an important happening. I went to Bordeaux in France to produce a "quickie book" about a new transmission plant when it was realized that this would be an effective way of achieving several PR objectives. One was the need to communicate to the local community that this major industrial development was being accomplished with sensitivity to controversial local environmental and other issues. A second PR need was to instill in French people pride and a sense of identity with a project being undertaken by an alien multinational company.

Also, there were subsidiaries in other countries who would take components from the plant and needed to be informed and motivated about the quality of its projects and the reasons why the Bordeaux location had been selected when some of them had wanted this prime project badly. Finally, there were customers and dealers who needed to be influenced to regard this new development and the accompanying technology in a positive way.

All these objectives were well met by a book that was quick and comparatively economical to produce and distribute. It took me about two weeks (the photographer spent only three days on the project) to finish the handsome, 80-page, large-format publication.

PR AND MARKETING TOOLS

Pennzoil and other oil companies have found that consumer handbooks work very well for them as PR and marketing tools. The Associated Electric Cooperative turned one of its annual reports into a book. Its theme, "there is no such thing as magic", involved creative night-time photography.

There are a lot of other examples. It always pays to consider the PR power of a book for a wide range of projects, including giving increased impact and corporate identification to sponsorships. If you keep to the paperbook format and do not get involved in the delays and expense of hard covers, books need not be inordinately expensive—but can be perceived as high-cost items by recipients.

Desktop publishing provides new ways of keeping down costs and speeding up the publishing process. We will look at examples of this later. Indeed, a book produced primarily for PR purposes can, if done well, cost nothing or even generate a profit.

A classic example of this was the Parker Pen Company's sponsored book *Do's and Taboos Around the World*, which has more than covered its costs by becoming a commercial success with more than 50,000 copies sold since September 1985. Based on research into international business protocol, it generated extensive media coverage, provided the basis for a slide program, became an attractive premium to sell pens, has been translated into a number of foreign languages, and has been picked up as a commercial title by various independent publishers as both a book and an audio book cassette.

One shrewd move in planning this strategy was to create the book as a product in its own right as well as being a publicity tool, which ensured that its costs could at least self-liquidate from sales revenue. An executive with considerable international business experience was assigned to the project as media spokesperson, a strategy that will help any image-building program with both domestic and international target audiences.

Shutting the Media up

How the South African government carried out an effective negative PR campaign by exploiting the laziness of the media

Journalists are, on the whole, basically lazy. If this were not so, the media could not be so easily manipulated by business and political interests who exploit this laziness by making it easy for reporters to cover what is good publicity and put obstacles in the way of writing stories about negative topics.

So news that is good (for companies and politicians) should be timed just right for major deadlines and be released with comprehensive press kits and carefully staged and convenient photographic opportunities. Bad news, such as a product recall or poor quarterly performance figures, is released by the professionals at the most awkward times for the media, with the minimum of hand-out material and the contacts for followup media enquiries conveniently out-of-town. Beware of the damage such tactics can do to long-term media relationships.

I remember one very embarrassing product recall that was released late on a holiday weekend to meet the statutory disclosure requirements but minimize media coverage. At the prior internal briefing, it was made clear to the PR staff involved that they should be well away from their telephones so that reporters could not reach them. This was a complete switch from the usual policy of always ensuring that at least one spokesperson was accessible at any time.

Media manipulation comes particularly to the foreground in civil wars, for instance, in the case of Hemingway and his contemporaries covering the Spanish Civil War and in more recent conflicts in Africa and Asia. The Biafra War, which caused such enormous bloodshed in Nigeria, was fought in the international media as well as through the towns and villages of Africa's most populous nation. I was covering one local action with a BBC television crew when the area commander ordered a temporary ceasefire while the cameraman ran off to get more film, so conscious were the Nigerians of the need to counter the Biafrans' very effective international publicity.

In that war, starving children were used as a PR vehicle to distort what was actually happening and to generate overseas publicity.

The most glaring and best documented example of a PR campaign designed to minimize coverage is the one that has been undertaken, with enormous success, by the South African government to limit international television reporting of violence in black townships. It is one of the few such cases which has been well quantified, and, unpalatable as it is, it provides many lessons.

CUTTING THE COVERAGE

Despite all the media battering it has taken over the years, the South African government is still not really battle-hardened to negative criticism and is very much aware of the damage that bad press does to its economic and other interests.

It therefore moved very decisively to counter daily incidents of violence involving black civil rights protesters, schoolchildren, and the unemployed, which made excellent international television news footage. Not since Vietnam had the American networks, in their battle for ratings, been able to tap an apparently inexhaustible supply of strong action clips to add spice and increase viewer interest.

Many of the riots, demonstrations and clashes with security forces were sad and genuine examples of the boiling frustration of the South African black community. However, a large number also were staged specifically for the television cameras as part of a well-orchestrated political PR campaign. The South African authorities, therefore, felt justified in clamping down on the activities of the foreign television crews. They were banned from going into the townships and filming a wide range of activities. Draconian reporting restrictions were imposed on the print media also.

The result was "The Great South African Disappearing Act". In the month before the regulations were imposed, news—almost entirely negative—about South Africa occupied 727.5 column inches in *the New York Times,* but only 402 inches in the month after the ban. Network television news coverage in the United States plummeted sharply also, with even greater benefit to the South African government.

DISAPPEARING ACT

"In a remarkable disappearing act, hard news about the South African unrest has simply fallen off the world's screen, " commented the distinguished former editor of the *Cape Times,* Anthony Head.

Without the high-impact reports of violence, South Africa soon declined in news value generally, much to the chagrin of the anti-apartheid organizations who had to work much harder to get coverage for their activities.

The South African government has demonstrated repeatedly that just by making it difficult for the media to cover events, it can often reduce to a comparative trickle the amount of negative publicity its policies receive. The overseas media simply move on to other, more easily covered, stories. With the exception of a minority of dedicated journalists, they do not pursue stories aggressively or work hard to overcome obstacles unless a story is really "hot" or exclusive.

One of the sad consequences of the disinvestment and withdrawal of leading American and European corporations from South Africa is that the alternative press there has lost much of the support it might have expected to receive from international companies, both from their placing of advertisements and from valuable support services their PR people offered to journalists.

Just as skilled PR people can achieve media coverage, so they can reduce the exposure for a sensitive or embarrassing topic, putting obstacles in the way of reporters, inhibiting the dissemination of an unpalatable announcement, and maybe even preventing a murky secret from ever being made public.

Sonoma State University's Project Censored uncovers considerable evidence of this every year in its annual survey of censored or underreported corporate, industrial and political stories. They are particularly concerned about forecasts that by the 1990s a handful of giant corporations will control most of the media in the United States.

Among the examples of media manipulation cited by the project are the number of unreported nuclear accidents around the world, a figure that results in the nuclear industry's having a suspect record for industrial safety; the United States and its Contra drug connection; biological warfare research; and the disposal of toxic wastes.

The Reporters' Committee for Freedom of the Press in 1987 issued a Media Alert documenting 135 instances which, it claimed, reflected attempts by the Reagan administration and its supporters to restrict editorial freedom or access to government information of public interest. The American Library Association annually updates its list of attempts by the administration to restrict government information.

Democracies really do not enjoy freedom of the press to the extent that we imagine, and that poses considerable ethical problems for PR people as well as for journalists.

Dictatorial regimes are even worse, and we will look later at some of the PR techniques that opposition groups are using to counter official propaganda.

Terrorists Make Brilliant Publicists

How the Shiite Amal terrorists controlled American network news and proved themselves to be masters of media manipulation

International terrorism has proved extremely adept at both making and directing news coverage. They can move faster than sophisticated governments, using all their resources to exploit PR opportunities, as the Iranians and their supporters delight in demonstrating.

For example, the 1985 hijacking of a TWA airliner en route to Beirut was part of a very well-orchestrated PR campaign. It is included here not so much as an example for corporate emulation, but more as a warning to all those concerned about the negative aspects of media manipulation.

In Beirut, with very limited resources, a group of street fighters effectively outwitted and controlled some of the highest paid reporters in the world for a period of 17 days, calling most of the shots in world coverage of the ordeal of the American hostages.

They set up a press room, dictated pool coverage on the television crews, staged events to ensure that the story would develop as they wanted it to, effectively distorted much of the coverage so as to enhance their own image, and obtained enormous amounts of publicity for their political objectives.

"The terrorists' media relations were so successful, they even were able to soften the repercussions of the brutal murder of passenger Robert Dean Stretham," commented the American Legal Foundation. "Media exposure has the power to turn individuals or terrorist factions with few members and little power into major players on the world stage."

Section 4

The Best PR Techniques Work Just as Well for Teddy Bears as They Do for Tarts

How you can give Hallmark a scare for under $5,000

Now there's a headline for you! Before we get into the case history of a talented young Californian who is living out many PR practitioners' dreams running his own publishing business, please take a moment to look again at the above heading. It is a model attention-grabber.

Some of the greatest missed opportunities in all forms of written communication arise from failing to exploit the headline, be it on a news release, an interoffice memo, or the title or chapter headings of a book.

Even the most experienced of us slip up sometimes in this respect, through laziness or the perceived need to be ponderous or serious because of the nature of the message, the medium, or the target audience.

I've just done it myself in a book about the fascinating worlds of faking, forging, counterfeiting, and product piracy. I wrote the book in a zippy style, trying to entertain as well as inform, and commissioned some lively, fun cartoon drawings for illustrations. Then, because I want my book to be taken seriously by art and antique dealers and collectors, I lost my nerve and agreed to a boring label title on the cover—*The Collector's Guide to Fakes and Forgeries*. It deserves a better title—and I should know better, too, after all these years of making my living out of marketing attention-grabbing words and phrases.

Every knowledgeable PR person—and all but unworldly, academic editors—know that a catchy headline and introduction are vital elements in any effective written communication. Clients have often argued with me about this, because they confuse high-impact, attention-getting literary devices with what they perceive to be the trivialization of ventures that for them are very serious.

A company spends a great deal of money developing a product on which perhaps its whole future—together with a number of jobs

In a nice PR touch, Frank Donadee sends out invoices and other communications accompanied by cards of bear drawings by his wife Maia, which are becoming very collectable.

Frank also uses high impact, attractive envelopes for his written communications. They really stand out from all the junk mail.

and career prospects—depend. Then a slick PR man comes along, is briefed thoroughly on the technical and marketing background of the project, and produces a media release reducing it to a few words of limited vocabulary and short simple sentences.

Managers often find that difficult to take, especially engineers and other technically orientated executives who are too close to the scientific brilliance of their new device or formula to live comfortably with attempts to project it in a lively, simple way.

TEN SECONDS TO IMPACT

But professional communicators know—and must in turn spread the message—that your media release may have a life of only 10 seconds or less when it emerges from the envelope, unless the heading and introduction hit the recipient straight between the eyes.

That's why Frank Donadee of Pomona, near Los Angeles, will let me get away with linking his charming teddy bears to the tarts who figured earlier in his career. Frank is a professional PR man who knows about such things—he even used his wedding to boost his business. We'll get to that later.

Actually, the link between the tarts and the teddies is somewhat tenuous, but, in following that golden rule of PR, *"Deliver on your promises"*, let us justify it immediately.

Frank began his PR career with the City of Los Angeles promoting an internal client list of about a dozen departments. One of his most successful campaigns was generating national attention for a welfare program in which prostitutes, female drug addicts, and other women of the streets of L.A. were turned into respectable members of a drill team. They toured the United States, and Frank's print, radio and TV publicity helped them both generate funding and act as valuable role models for other young women in trouble.

The lessons learned on that campaign and other city social projects, such as painting murals on the walls of buildings in the rougher parts of L.A. to deter vandalism, helped Frank a lot when he set up his own publishing business.

BIG RESULTS FROM SMALL BEGINNINGS

He started with a mere $300 in capital, raised by selling his battered Volkswagen bus. In seven years, the enterprise has grown to be worth around a half-million dollars, thanks to a talented wife, desktop publishing technology, and good PR. Here's the story—an eye-opener on how the little things count for a lot in good public relations and what a potent weapon the new desktop publishing systems can be for all of us in the communication business.

Frank began his publishing enterprise with a modest, local, free newspaper that struggled for survival against lack of capital and local awareness. It rarely appeared on time because of antiquated production systems. Turning points were his marriage and a Macintosh computer.

Much of the business in Pomona stems from its popularity as a center for antiques, so Frank's paper naturally started to concentrate on this aspect of local trade. He exploited both the interest in antiques and a hot community issue when he and his bride partner, art director Maia, made their marriage a major local media event.

Brought up in Hollywood, Frank is a movie buff, but that was not the only reason he chose to get married in the art deco Pomona movie theater. The future of the theater had become a controversial political issue. It had degenerated into a flea pit showing low grade Spanish features and was threatened with closure, demolition or conversion into a community center.

Frank and Maia got married there in period costume, arriving in a magnificent horse-drawn carriage. They generated a great deal of media coverage by exploiting the newsworthiness of the venue and the human interest and picture opportunities inherent in a wedding. They were the story, but their business got the exposure. They also overcame one of the biggest PR challenges there is—to get publications to provide positive exposure for a rival.

SMOOTH IMAGE CHANGE

Local awareness of them and their business increased, advertising revenue went up, and the image change from a community-oriented,

Frank and Maia Donadee made even their wedding work for them as a PR vehicle and followed up by using illustrations of the event in their publication.

free sheet to a quality paper specializing in the antique trade went off smoothly.

"But you cannot do something like that purely as a publicity stunt and make it as successful," Frank emphasizes. "Our target audience was our local community and we were part of that community, so our marriage was a valid local event, even if we did go all out to make it high exposure with commercial objectives."

Circulation of their paper rose to 11,000 and advertising revenue quadrupled during the next few years of steady growth—in which Maia's teddy bears played a very important part.

Maia has a talent for drawing delightful bear illustrations and these started creeping into the paper, now called *The Collector*. The same bear figures were used to add a more human, friendly touch to the bills sent out for advertising and subscriptions.

MAKE PEOPLE SMILE

"We find enclosing bear cards with invoices and business correspondence very cost-effective public relations," says Frank. "The bears make people smile, they are friendly and, although we cannot quantify it, I am convinced that they help us to get paid more promptly."

Readers and customers urged Frank and Maia to use the bears to get into the greeting card business, but that became feasible only when they purchased their first Macintosh computer.

"It transformed my business," says Frank. "Getting into desktop publishing is the best move any publisher, public relations consultancy or other business needing printed communications can make.

"The Macintosh gave us control over our newspaper. We no longer had to rely on typesetters, who frequently caused us to miss deadlines when they were late with our material. Plus the Mac allowed us to create far superior layouts in about a third of the time. This has freed us to get into new businesses."

Very quickly, Frank and Maia developed a selection of 370 greetings cards, 130 of these featuring the teddy bears (which sell at three times the rate of the others). Using the Mac—with *Ready, Set, Go* and *Pagemaker* software—he sent out media releases to locations throughout the United States, each accompanied by a bear illustration, which both increased their acceptability to editors and added to the impact when they were published.

GROWING WITH SPIN-OFFS

The Mac also made it economical to produce a catalogue of the bear cards, which now goes out to 4,000 people on a mailing list built from the editorial exposure and a modest advertising effort in collector magazines. The business continues to grow, with a new spin-off the development of a range of Teddy Bear Software—computer programs that enable bear enthusiasts to create and customize their own visuals.

"We really started something from nothing and it was PR which enabled us to do it," Frank says. "At the beginning we could not afford to advertise but, because we had something interesting to say, we were able to use low cost PR techniques to get us going.

THANK YOU, COMPUTERS

"Thanks to computers, computerized mailing lists, and high-quality photocopiers, it is now possible to get into publishing for a $5,000 investment and, with some good PR to start the marketing, perhaps even throw a scare into Hallmark."

Now that he has an established, influential journal, Frank finds himself on the receiving end of many press releases and points to both the wastage and the missed opportunities in so much PR related to the collecting/antique/art business.

"I get bombarded with releases from auctioneers, art galleries and companies—or their agencies—pushing collecting-related products," he says. "The vast majority reflect no knowledge of our paper and so it is a waste of time and money sending them to me. I use only editorial which I feel will benefit our 50,000 readers, virtually all of whom are located in Southern California and the majority of them actually involved in the antique trade in one way or another.

WASTEFUL PR MATERIAL

"Most of the PR material I receive does not meet these basic parameters and I get a lot of expensively generated photographs despite the fact that *The Collector* never uses halftones. We avoid the expense and the problems of unsatisfactory reproduction of photographs by sticking exclusively to line drawings. That gives us a publication with a quality appearance at a low cost."

So most of the PR material Frank receives is thrown away immediately. Even an attention grabbing headline isn't going to work with him—or any other editor, for that matter—unless the content is relevant to his publication.

At the same time, like many editors, Frank is always hungry for relevant releases.

"I'm always looking for interesting stories about antique stores in Southern California," he says, "but most owners seem too lazy or too ignorant about the fundamentals of PR practices to publicize their businesses."

Desktop Publishing as a PR Tool
How a politician with a PR problem became Mayor of San Francisco

Just as Frank Donadee's business would never have got over its initial problems without desktop publishing, so Art Agnos might never have been elected major of San Francisco if his PR man had not taken a Mac and a laser printer into his life.

This case history is a classic trend-setting example of how combining creative PR and desktop publishing can win an election.

This case history is a classic trend-setting example of how combining creative PR and desktop publishing can win an election. The Agnos campaign got into big trouble five months before polling day as a result of a wave of negative publicity about the candidate. The situation was turned around and enabled Agnos to win the confidence of the voters in a highly cost-effective way by using a desktop publishing system to generate a modest 82-page book called *Getting Things Done: Visions and Goals for San Francisco*, written by Agnos.

The book had a perceived value that made it far less likely to get thrown away than conventional, less-substantial, publicity material. Also, it was a uniquely effective medium in which Agnos could express his views on a wide range of important local issues.

HIGH IMPACT, LOW COST

Using a Mac computer and Microsoft Word and Pagemaker software, the book was typeset on a modest laser printer, and a quarter-of-a-million copies were printed on low-cost newspaper stock for a total cost of around $60,000. The Agnos campaign staff distributed the book door-to-door to voters, and the impact was equivalent in reach to a television campaign costing at least four times as much and probably not nearly as effective in terms of impact.

"His method of reaching voters quickly and cheaply turned out to be a brilliant tactical move," commented the editor-in-chief of *Publish!* magazine, David Bunnell, in an editorial.

"*Getting Things Done* is a terrific example of how the technology can be used as a tool to change the political process. The ability to turn out fliers, brochures and booklets so quickly and economically is as significant a development for candidates as television.

"In fact, I would venture to say that desktop publishing is sparking a rebirth of the political pamphlet. . . . What if presidential candidates distributed 100 million books that really explain their views and proposals? That tactic might just swing an election."

DESKTOP PUBLISHING TO CREATE NEW MEDIA

A growing number of communications professionals are demonstrating that desktop publishing makes it possible to create new media specific to particular needs for the effective dissemination of PR messages. It is now within comparatively modest budgets—and critical time frames—to produce slick, professional magazines, newspapers, or even books to get your point across very cost-efficiently.

However, Frank Donadee sounds several warnings. The editorial content must be strong—it's no good producing a beautiful book that nobody wants to read. And the other production costs—those incurred away from the desktop computer system—and the distribution system must be effective also. He gets 11,000 copies of *The Collector* distributed in about four days for an amazingly low cost of $600 by using a carefully coordinated system combining UPS, bulk mailing, and a part-time employee hand-delivering to outlets in the immediate locality.

Also, by not getting carried away by the technology, Frank keeps his print bill down to a typical $2,500 for a 40-page issue (standard 11-inch × 17-inch page size) with full color on the front and back as well as on six interior pages, plus four pages of spot color. By using only Maia's line drawings and no halftones, he gets excellent reproduction quality on low-cost newspaper stock. Careful selection of type styles gives a crisp look to copy printed with his desktop laser typesetter. Anyway, the cheap paper would not do justice to far more expensive, higher-resolution phototypesetting.

Particularly clever is the way that Maia uses color. There are no expensive separations; she generates the color, with the help of

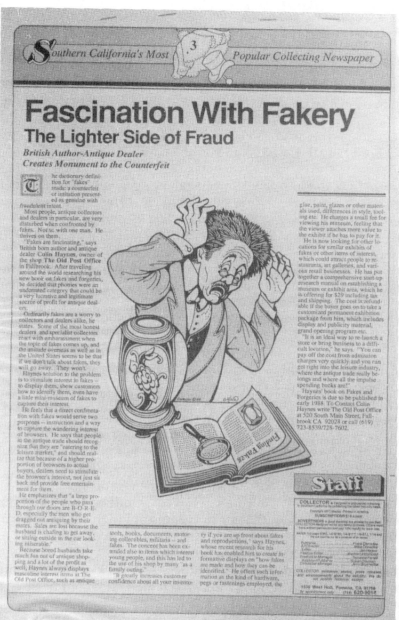

Desktop publishing is a powerful and ever-evolving medium, but PR people need to prepare and present their media material in ways that make it easier-to-handle for publishers using such systems. This page from *The Collector* newspaper shows what even a very small publishing house can do with imagination, a Mac, and a laser printer. It also gives me an excuse for plugging my last book, *Fakes and Forgeries*—you wouldn't expect a PR man to pass up such an opportunity, would you?

131

the computer in some instances, in the form of overlays that add little more to the production cost than making up an additional black-and-white plate.

SPOT COLOR EFFECTIVE

The use of a single spot color on some pages, with varying degrees of tinting by the simple use of screens of different density, is very effective, but so many publishers, even experienced ones, fail to liven up their pages in this way. Novice desktop publishers often get carried away by their access to a wide range of fonts and yet do not properly exploit the ability to generate graphics, when simple graphic solutions are often the best way of communicating facts.

KEEP IT SIMPLE

Graphic designers give sound advice when they urge newcomers to page layout to keep it simple and not let the technology take over.

You can get better quality setting and a more pleasing look by leaving columns justified only on the left, with a ragged right, rather than by pushing the still-limited abilities of desktop publishing systems to produce first-rate spacing, hyphenation and right justification.

Frank maintains that the strength of desktop publishing lies in its ability to quickly and inexpensively produce moderate-quality graphic material. This facility is most useful in low-budget projects with comparatively short runs.

A presidential candidate wanting to turn out 100 million copies of his manifesto would be well advised to stick with conventional typesetting because of the way in which the cost would be amortized over a long run.

"To print the Mayor of San Francisco's book in that quantity would cost perhaps $24 million. With a budget of that size it would not be advisable to try to save a couple of thousand dollars on typesetting. If it costs $5,000 for a top notch typesetter and only $1,000 for a desktop publisher, the percentage of the overall job is insignificant.

"Traditional typesetting would cost $.000208333 per unit, against $.0000416 to use desktop publishing. This is hardly a convincing argument for desktop publishing."

Frank points out that a political manifesto usually does not require great speed, being largely the thoughts and opinions developed over a lifetime. It would be extremely unusual if the few days saved by desktop publishing would be a great advantage over the traditional methods of book publishing.

SPEED AND LOW COST

"The kind of situation that would show off desktop publishing to its fullest advantage would be where speed and low cost masters are crucial," says Frank.

"Let us suppose that the mayor of a small town wanted to influence 100 of the city's community leaders who represent a wide cross section of civic, religious and business interests. He could make ten different versions of the same newsletter by just changing the lead story and a couple of the graphics, such as charts and graphs.

"The financial community could get one that featured a story about banks. The social service directors could read about new grants. Business owners could read about new code enforcement programs, etc. Every group could have a newsletter that prominently featured something that interested them.

EASY TO CUSTOMIZE INFORMATION

"Using traditional typesetting and layout and paste-up techniques, this would be a very expensive and time consuming task. It would not be worth so much effort for so few copies. However, with desktop publishing it would be easy to add and delete, highlight and obscure information."

The message, then, is to use the magic of desktop publishing in PR and other information-disseminating activities to which it is appropriate, but keep the technology in perspective and do the sums carefully.

Section 5

Selling the Royals
The media launching of Prince Charles

You might not think that the most famous royal family in the world would need a professional public relations officer, but the House of Windsor and the "product" it promotes—Britain—have benefitted on a number of occasions from PR expertise.

Indeed, shrewd professional PR advice was instrumental in changing media perception of Prince Charles from "a chinless wonder with big ears" to a widely respected media megastar, the world's most eligible bachelor, and a promotional vehicle worth millions of dollars to British tourism and world trade.

As a result of having communications professionals at his elbow since his youth, Prince Charles has avoided the often hostile relationships that resulted from his father's high-handed attitude toward the media. As a young reporter in England, I bought my first car from the proceeds of free-lance news items about the royal family, and one of my most abiding memories of those days is the withering look I got from the Duke of Edinburgh when I accidently got in his way while he was visiting a military installation.

His uncle, the Duke of Windsor, was not very considerate to reporters and photographers either, and the Abdication Affair, in which he gave up the throne to marry an American divorcee, was one of the most botched-up historic events ever from the PR point of view, despite the efforts of communicator *par excellence* Winston Churchill to handle it more perceptively.

Prince Charles was, in contrast, trained to treat the media with courtesy and to cooperate with them without losing his dignity or damaging the image of the Crown. He is a serious man, basically very shy, and the skillful PR handling he has received ensures that he is projected in a consistently positive way through the media.

EVEN THE ROYALS REHEARSE

There have been private, little-publicized sessions during which media people have had the opportunity to get to know Prince Charles on an informal level. There were even "practice press conferences", at which Prince Charles rehearsed handling media queries by working with trainee journalists. The Buckingham Palace Press Office departed radically from tradition by encouraging the media to have specialist correspondents with whom the royal family could build a relationship of mutual trust and cooperation, so as to "market" the Prince effectively and to subtly modify the perceptions of the Queen, Prince Phillip, and their children to be more in tune with the times.

In many respects, Prince Charles was promoted the way that an important new product is launched. The campaign provides a unique example of skillful PR at a very high level. The strength of the image created—and the Prince's own qualities—have been of lasting benefit during more recent, difficult episodes in his life, such as the death of a member of his skiing party (after which he could have been exposed to far more hostile press comment than he received), his marital problems, and his sometimes ill-conceived remarks about architecture and other major issues.

Some of the other members of the royal family, Britain's most prestigious PR asset, have not been as well served in the image business. The younger members of the family, notably the Duke and Duchess of York, have come across as being superficial partygoers, more like showbiz personalities than diplomatic and commercial ambassadors.

ILL-CONCEIVED PR

For example, it proved ill-conceived PR for the younger royals to become involved in televised high jinks in a series of glorified party games, and the 1988 visit of the Duke and Duchess of York to California, which could have done wonders to promote commerce and investment between the United States and Britain, woefully failed to achieve those objectives.

The Duke and his "Fergie" were nicknamed "The Rollicking Royals" as they romped through an American tour with precious little dignity, excruciating fashion sense, and thoughtless—often stupid—public utterances. A corporate PR practitioner would want to shoot any executives who behaved like that in public. Even the pseudoroyalty of Hollywood showbiz personalities who hosted the British visitors came across as having more dignity and substance. Joan Collins looked more like a Duchess than did Fergie when they were introduced.

As a result, much of the media coverage was awful. Queen Elizabeth, a shrewd woman with excellent PR sense, was reportedly not in the least amused.

"Here we go again—genuflecting, curtsying and shamelessly salivating like brainless bloodhounds all because a couple of royal ribbon cutters have decided to pompously romp through Los Angeles," commented the Los Angeles *Herald Examiner,* which thought the Yorks displayed "no pomp and very little circumstance."

CRITICAL MEDIA

The British media were even more critical with their negative PR comments.

"While the stars of Hollywood dressed in discreet black and stayed in the shadows, down the stairs walloped someone who looked as if she'd just won third prize for her Carmen Miranda impersonation in an end-of-the-pier show," wrote Craig Brown in the *London Sunday Times* of the Hollywood reception for the royal couple.

"Trotting next to her was an over-animated young man with a carnivorous grin who, no matter how many dinner jackets he wore, would still look like a Third Division footballer out for a good time at The Hippodrome. Yes, the Duke and Duchess of Yob had come to town."

Such ridicule was directed at a couple who started off with such strong PR potential that 500 million people around the world tuned in to watch their wedding on television. Not only was there a failure to capitalize on royal charisma for valid commercial objectives, the expensive royal PR exercise proved seriously counterproductive.

PROTECTING IMAGES

There are lessons here that can be applied in a number of PR situations. Despite the charisma and communications skills the leaders of corporations and other organizations may have, their images need careful nurturing and protection. One slip and the damage could be permanent. Consider Lyndon Johnson photographed holding a dog by the ears and Prime Minister Margaret Thatcher looking ridiculous as she chased garbage across St. James's Park in an ill-planned media photocall to publicize the problem of littering. The examples are legion.

Perhaps the most carefully nurtured image in American corporate life is that of Chrysler chairman Lee Iaccocca, a born showman who nevertheless carefully preserves a persona of authority and trustworthiness even through such traumas as having the publicity spotlight focussed on losing his job and on his marital problems.

Real-life personalities play an important role in many aspects of PR and they, and their communications advisors, need to be constantly on the alert to nurture and protect their images, just as that same professional expertise is deployed on product and corporate images. But, just as you cannot forever maintain a strong, positive image for a rotten company or product, nor can you indefinitely inflate a basically inferior person into heroic proportions by using PR techniques.

Being the PR person behind a celebrity is a particularly demanding role requiring great patience and sensitivity. I salute those who do it well.

Early in my PR career, I was interviewed for a job that involved the effective promotion of a figurehead boss. I suggested that one positive image–building action might be if he bought a new suit to replace the shapeless, shiny outfits he usually wore. It was unsubtle and my timing was awful, so I deserved not to get the job. Salt was rubbed into the wound when the successful candidate did manage to get the client to dress more appropriately, but only after he was engaged and had established the relationship that enabled him to make—and to get accepted—such critical personal recommendations.

Computers Are a Wonderful PR Tool
Even revolutionaries use them

The opponents of dictatorial regimes are getting smarter to counter censorship and other oppressive measures. Let us salute those public relations people who are using all kinds of communications techniques in the most adverse circumstances to disseminate messages of the freedom that many of us in democratic societies take for granted.

COUNTERING CAPTIONS

A particularly imaginative and technologically advanced campaign is being waged by the Polish underground. They have overcome many of the practical problems of stringent government controls over freedom of speech by exploiting computer technology—with lessons from which we might draw in different ways.

Polish Solidarity members were involved in a really imaginative project that enabled viewers of the state monopoly television broadcasting services to get the opposition as well as the government viewpoints. Using a cheap microcomputer, a transmitter, and remarkable technical ingenuity, the underground fed their call for a boycott of elections into the government television service in the form of captions that appeared on Polish television screens.

They also used their computer skills to monitor the elections and demonstrate that the government lied about the results. This was a tremendous PR coup and has long-term implications in demonstrating how, even under the most authoritarian regimes, the state need not have a monopoly of information important to the society.

UNDERGROUND PUBLISHING

In Poland and other countries, computers are being used to revolutionize underground publishing. Information can be stored and moved around far more safely on diskettes than it can as printing on paper. Even the less-sophisticated word processing software and hardware can give to the people communication power far in excess of their traditional information-disseminating weapons—typewriters and mimeograph machines.

I was at the 1988 Newsletter Association annual conference in Washington when we all responded to an impassioned appeal to send a photocopier to a leading Soviet dissident whose primitive publishing equipment had been confiscated by the authorities. We should have sent him a personal computer and a printer as well; then he would have had the basic equipment which has made self-publishing such an exciting communications field in the West.

THE PC REVOLUTION

The personal computer revolution is of vital importance to all of us in the public relations business in many ways. It is important to ensure in some campaigns that your information is available on electronic databases. Often this will happen automatically if your material is published by the many newspapers and magazines, such as those operated by the Dow Jones organization in the United States and the *Financial Times* in Europe, that now put their material on databases.

Use these databases also for your research, to dig up quickly facts that can be used to amplify and add background to almost any media release material.

Also, the value of your media services can increase if you make your editorial submissions available in electronic form, either by transmitting them directly via modem into the electronic editing systems of your target publications or by physically sending diskettes compatible with the publication's systems. However, the advent of computer viruses has made the exchange of disks a rather risky business.

GET YOUR HARDWARE INTO THE FIELD

Don't be afraid to take your word processing out in the field to give a fast media service at special events. I have done this very successfully under the most adverse conditions; for a cross-country riding contest and an automotive record-breaking attempt sponsored by a client.

My PR team and I loaded our ordinary office computers and printers into the backs of our cars, set them up in a tent, and produced immaculate media releases on the spot within minutes of information coming in. Now, I would not run the press office for a major event, especially one with fast-breaking developments such as a sports sponsorship, without having computerized word processing facilities available. The new generation of laptop computers makes this much easier to achieve.

In many cases, these facilities should include a telephone modem link with the main office for the speedy and efficient handling back at base of material that needs to be disseminated widely to media not actually covering the action on the spot.

Personal computers played an important behind-the-scenes PR roll in the 1988 U.S. presidential primaries, further demonstrating their mobility as well as their efficiency. They are now becoming a key element in many PR activities, but don't limit their application to fixed office installation. Take all that communication power with you whenever you can use it effectively.

EVEN SIMPLE, CHEAP EQUIPMENT CAN PRODUCE GOOD PR

Despite what all the advertisements and magazines are proclaiming, most PR applications do not need expensive sophisticated equipment. If the budget is really tight, you can be up and running with used equipment and simple word processing software for a few hundred dollars.

If you are starting from scratch with $1,000 or $2,000 to spend, an IBM PC compatible desktop computer, preferably with a hard disk and drive for both the standard diskette and the smaller and more durable micro floppy diskettes, is a good choice. The selection of a printer is vital. A laser printer is ideal, starting at around $1,600, but you also will get good results—if more slowly and less flexibly—from any of the many daisy wheel printers now available at a fraction of that cost. Do not use a dot matrix printer, except for internal drafts.

The quality of the hard copy is much inferior to that generated by laser or impact printers such as the daisy wheel. Increasingly, editors will not handle dot matrix printed copy because they claim it causes eye strain.

The desk top outfit is complemented by a laptop portable, but make sure you get one that really is compatible with your main office system.

MAC VERSUS PC

More writers and PR people are using the Macintosh computers these days, especially for desktop publishing. The initial investment, though, is higher than for PC clones, and it pays to try one out for a reasonable period to decide if you can live with the small monochrome screen and keyboard. I find it much easier to work on a large color monitor with a bigger keyboard, even if the PC system is more complicated to learn.

With either the PC or the Mac systems, the mouse is a useful tool to speed up editing.

Your mailing lists are much easier to handle—and keep up to date—on a computer. An important PR tool found in the better word processing programs is the mail merge facility, which enables you to churn out personalized letters to media contacts, increasing the impact of your material when it hits the journalist's desk.

SPELLING CHECKERS

A spelling checker is an invaluable tool also, especially if you work alone and do not have someone else to proofread your copy. There is special software available that will actually carry out limited editing, highlighting clumsy phrasing, repetition and grammatical mistakes. The early versions were not very impressive, but the technology is improving all the time, and inexperienced writers may find editing programs useful tools, although not substitutes for creative quality.

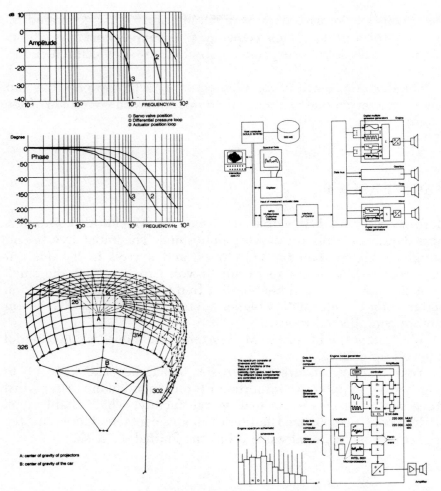

Computer graphics are great for generating visuals for media kits and other applications. Daimler-Benz has used them in all kinds of applications promoting its advanced technology in the driving simulator that recreates road conditions in the company's Berlin research establishment.

How to Produce a Customized Company Magazine
With the least hassle and the most dazzle

New electronic publishing technology now makes it possible to produce employee publications far more cost-effectively than ever before.

These publications can be a shocking waste of money, if they are like the vast number of mediocre in-house newsletters, newspapers, and magazines produced around the world. In contrast, the good examples are practical tools for Human Resource and PR Departments to help them market company philosophies and objectives to their employees in a highly cost-effective way.

It is a big mistake to think that employee publications should be limited to just one company newspaper, magazine or newsletter. There is a wide variety of formats, each most applicable to a given situation, as some of the examples later in this chapter indicate.

Particularly consider the use of special publications to achieve specific objectives. The following composite example drawn from a number of actual case histories illustrates how one could address the twin objectives of reducing labor turnover and of achieving greater support for training programs.

"ADVANCEMENT NEWS"

The biggest single reason most employees leave their jobs is dissatisfaction with advancement opportunities, according to a recent Adia poll of personnel decision makers.

Also, the biggest waste of resources and expenditure in many companies is the underutilization of training facilities and programs, coupled with the additional loss that occurs when expensively trained employees leave because of dissatisfaction with advancement opportunities.

To tackle this issue, you recommend that management launch a new publication called *Advancement News.* You could use the existing company newspaper, but perhaps it does not enjoy a very good reputation, has become rather boring, and, over the years, has come to be regarded as a mouthpiece for management.

DEFINE OBJECTIVES

First of all, define your objectives. You want *Advancement News* to do two main things, and all other considerations should be secondary to these objectives.

1. Give employees a more positive attitude toward their advancement prospects in the organization.
2. Motivate them to make better use of training resources.

If these objectives are met, the company benefits from improved morale, reduction in turnover, and a better return from training programs. Quantify these benefits to get support from all areas of management and obtain a sensible budget allocation so that you can do a decent job.

Now, build your editorial philosophy. *Advancement News* is, above all, a service to employees, and everything in it must be written from the viewpoint of this target audience, just as if they were subscribers to be wooed to a commercial publication. Only with this sympathy to the needs and aspirations of the audience can you achieve the corporate objectives of demonstrating every month (or however frequently the newsletter is published) that the company is dedicated to advancing the careers of its people. Do not speak from the company viewpoint; doing so makes it more difficult to come across with sincerity and motivate employees about training opportunities so that the company can make every dollar in its training budget and improve the organization's return from its human resources.

CUSTOMIZE PUBLICATIONS

The continual developments in electronic publishing make it practical to exactly customize such a publication to meet your internal communication needs and budget. If the formula isn't working as well as it might, then you have the flexibility to modify it rapidly and at low cost on the computer. However, beware of confusing your audience by constant changes in style, content, and design—and never introduce changes just because some new fancy computer software tempts you to try a variety of typographical tricks. The old journalistic KISS maxim applies especially to desktop publishing—"Keep It Simple, Stupid".

Advancement News should contain lots of real-life, personal, human-interest stories about employees who have benefited—by advancement and perhaps in other, less-tangible, ways—because of the opportunities for career development the company offers. Maintain a strong editorial theme motivating employees to support training programs of all kinds, letting real examples underline the message without any need to preach or moralize.

If there are valid reasons why you cannot generate enough copy internally, *Advancement News* could also carry strong motivational copy of a more general nature about the benefits of career development and training from outside sources, including editorial syndicates, commercial companies operating in that field, and any consultants your HR department may be using.

EXPLOIT CONSULTANTS WITHOUT PAYING THEM

House journal editors rarely exploit the consultants called into an organization. These people usually are very pleased to produce special articles that demonstrate their expertise and can be very authoritative—if the consultants are good. Don't let them "hard sell" their own organizations—just adding a credit line listing them as the source, with a brief description of their background to put them in perspective, should be enough. However, there is merit in letting them quote their own successes in other companies to show that your organization employs quality people to help it—and its own people—progress.

If your editorial resources are very limited, then you can draw heavily on copy contributed from outside and still customize the publication with a masthead exclusively identifying it with your company. Just as a commercial newspaper does, insert fliers about your own programs. This is a low-cost way of tailoring your newsletter to the needs of limited sections of your circulation list. For example, you could insert a flier about a pilot program only in the copies going to members of the department or to the plant where that program is being tested.

One practical way of customizing is to have your own editorial on the front and back pages and the center spread and to use more general material to fill other pages. This cost-effectively produces a professional, substantial publication entirely identified with your company.

You can contract other professionals to perform all or part of the production. You assume in-house responsibility for those editorial tasks you are equipped to do or for which you wish to retain direct responsibility.

CREATE AN ELECTRONIC PACKAGE

If you are serving a large group, consider delivering the publication as an electronic desktop publishing package to different plants, subsidiaries, and so forth. Their own in-house staff can adapt it to their varying needs in a fraction of the time they would spend to produce such a publication from scratch themselves, and at far less cost.

You could even deliver the publication to them in the form of camera-ready art with blanks into which they can easily insert their own editorial items using an office word processor—even a typewriter. This format can both be professional in appearance and have high impact. You can see the technique used in *Newsweek* and *U.S. News & World Report* when they use typewriter typefaces for a "hot", newsletter-type section. Even a modest in-house printing department can undertake the final production if as much preliminary work as possible is done for them.

Health News could be a similar publication, devoted to informing your employees about company medical and other health-care programs. It could be particularly effective for companies offering discretionary medical packages of the "cafeteria" type, in which employees need a lot of information so that they can construct the medical aid program most appropriate to their individual needs and so make best use of discretionary-benefits schemes.

Such special publications are very cost-effective in developing programs aimed at improving the health of employees—helping to mitigate the steep increases in the cost of employee medical schemes, one of the biggest concerns of CEOs at this time. Some of the firms supplying health programs produce magazines aimed at employees, which you can customize to your own needs by using some of the techniques I have suggested.

You can tailor publications to other internal-communication needs. Examples include *Suggestion News, Quality News, Safety News,* and so on.

PRODUCTION NIGHTMARES

Although company newspapers and magazines are often the most effective medium for communicating with employees, they can be a staffing and administration nightmare. Don't move unless you have a well thought-out action plan that goes way beyond the initial issue and has the budget allocation to ensure that you can maintain a publication that really works and does not trail off into mediocrity or cease to come out regularly. If there is one thing worse than not communicating with employees, it is starting to communicate and then stopping. Your organization's credibility goes right out the window if you cannot keep the momentum going.

The Power of Newsletters
Create your own medium

Newsletters are an increasingly important medium that PR people may tend not to take as seriously as the subscribers who pay dearly for the information they contain. There are probably 3,000 different commercial newsletters and another 10,000 from professional and trade associations published in the United States alone. That does not include the many newsletters put out locally by various groups or internal company publications. Newsletters are a powerful communication medium which should always be considered when formulating your PR strategy.

You can even create your own newsletter if you find it difficult to get your information disseminated to your target audiences through existing media. Many organizations now produce, for both external and internal audiences, newsletters of various kinds that perform a valuable PR role. Some are separate publishing-profit centers in their own right. Or they may be natural spin-offs from corporate activities which generate information suitable to put into newsletters to distribute free to prospective customers and other contacts for promotional purposes.

If you produce a newsletter that claims to be an authoritative source for information on a topic or industry, make sure it has the editorial standards—particularly impartiality and balanced coverage—that are essential for conventional independent publications.

A ROUTE TO OTHER MEDIA

A newsletter is also a route to being quoted in other media. Many journalists seem to have no problem quoting a newsletter as a source but often are reluctant to attribute a quote to a company expert. You may spend an hour on the phone giving information to a journalist who then publishes much of it without giving you or your organization any credit.

An impressive example of the publicity power of newsletters is the work done by Pete Packer as a one-man PR department for the Winsconsin consultancy firm of Runzheimer International. They publish seven management newsletters on travel and living costs, and Pete uses them very effectively as PR vehicles for his organization, averaging over 100 clippings and 40 media interviews a month.

"Seventy-five to eighty percent of the work I do is based on the newsletters we produce, although they are a small segment of the company," he says. "Newsletters are a natural source of news and have instant credibility with the media who do not see any conflict with their interests in attributing information to a newsletter by name."

Pete Packer has a professional philosophy that I applaud and that contributes much to his success—he regards himself as an extension of the media working within his own organization. He approaches his task from the viewpoint and needs of his target audience, his journalist contacts, constantly moving through his organization asking questions and reading documentation, then sitting down and writing that information up as if he were a reporter on one of his target newspapers.

LOW SELF-ESTEEM

That is in contrast to the attitude of so many PR people who have low self-esteem and are therefore treated as they behave—as the lackeys of management.

Other tips from Pete include making sure that all your key editorial contacts are on the complimentary mailing list for your newsletters, recognizing that the cost to you is very small but the return from being quoted can be very high. Also, most journalists do not have budgets that permit them to subscribe to newsletters; if you do not give them complimentary copies, they almost certainly will not see your newsletters at all.

If you are starting up a newsletter—or producing one already—remember that this is a unique form of publishing with the emphasis on information that your readers feel they really need to know, presented in a very concise, easily digested form. Rather like radio, it should come across as a one-to-one communication exercise between you and the other person.

DON'T BE TOO SLICK

Don't make the presentation too glossy and slick. A large proportion of the most successful newsletters are very simply produced, often in typewriter fonts with ragged-right formatting rather like interoffice memos, to enhance the perception of one-to-one inside information. I know of successful publishers with sophisticated computer systems who still turn out the masters for their newsletters on old daisy wheel printers so as to make them appear typewritten, even if the circulation is several thousand.

If you are generating newsworthy material of considerable sub-stance and greater length than is appropriate for the newsletter for-mat, consider issuing it as a special report. Instead of just a news release, turn your material into an event with the publication of a special report, even if your only target is the media. Announce the report as an important event, even if it comes from a commercial company and not an independent organization, and send it out to the media along with a release summarizing the main newsworthy points you want to get across.

The modern computer, photocopier, and in-house binding sys-tems make it comparatively easy and economical to publish impres-sive special reports and newsletters if the information is on hand. Both can be powerful PR tools if used imaginatively.

Electronic Editing Tips
Technology is no substitute for creativity

Old dogs find it hard to learn new tricks, but most veteran communicators have found it much easier than expected to adapt to the electronic editing age. If you write a lot and have not yet made the switch to computerized word processing, you have a great treat in store.

For a start, the physical effort is significantly less than working on an electric typewriter, let alone a manual one. Among my store of useless information is the statistic that a productive typist working hard for a day expends enough energy pounding the keys to lift an elephant two inches off the ground. In contrast, your fingers flick effortlessly over the computer keyboard, and thoughts seem to become words without any physical energy being expended.

You can then sort, correct, and rearrange those words quickly and proficiently, checking your spelling and instantly being offered a whole variety of layout options. When I fell behind schedule and had to churn out several episodes of a romantic serial for a pulp magazine very quickly, 8,000 words a day were nowhere near as physically tiring as half that number typed on a conventional typewriter would have been.

Even if you are familiar with electronic editing, though, there are still several tips I have garnered from writers in the PR business that you may find of benefit.

HARD COPY PROOFING

One of the most important is not to do the final proofreading of copy on the screen, however high a resolution your monitor gives you. You do spot more errors if you double-space the text, but even then mistakes seem to slip past you far more easily than when you check hard copy (printed on paper). Of course, it is always much better to get someone else who is fresh to your copy to check it; you seem to read through without realizing the gremlins that have crept into your own words.

The spell-checking programs are a real blessing, especially those with comprehensive dictionaries in which you can save technical words and proper nouns that you use frequently. A thesaurus can be useful also. However, I use dictionary programs only for spelling checks. Any reasonably literate PR person who has to look up a word in the dictionary to find out what it means is using the wrong word in virtually all release material, with the possible exception of some special terms in copy for technical magazines.

The better word processors have macrowriting facilities, and you can save a lot of time if you learn how to use them. They will manipulate text to fit into your previously defined formats and also will search for and replace words that are wrong or conflict with your editorial practice (e.g., certain abbreviations or capitalization).

COMPUTERIZED RESEARCH

Use the computer to search for information from one of the many databases now available. That facility alone justifies spending $100–$200 on a telephone modem, which allows you to transmit and receive data over an ordinary telephone line.

The modem also opens up the real benefits to be gained by receiving copy quickly from free lances or staff away from the office, without the need to rekeyboard it. You also can send your own release material directly to publications, so that they can handle it most conveniently and efficiently.

However, do not use fancy formatting, such as bold, italic, and underlined words. Most publications don't use these techniques to give emphasis to words or phrases; the writing and sentence structure should be good enough in themselves to convey your meaning and emphasis.

STORING AND TRANSFERRING DATA

Remember to save, in ASCII code, files that you need to move between compatible computer systems that have different word processing software. In most software, this merely means saving the text with the filename followed by a ".ASC" definition. There is software that will allow varying degrees of interchange between C/PM, Mac and IBM PC systems.

Always back up your files and keep a spare diskette containing important material in a separate place. Don't just dump everything onto the hard disk in the belief that it will always be there for instant recall. Hard disks do have problems; if they crash, you may lose everything on them.

If you do run into trouble, call the help lines provided by the more responsible manufacturers of both software and hardware. They can be remarkably helpful. If all else fails, try switching on and off—this low-tech approach can be surprisingly effective, although you will lose your current work unless you have saved it.

LOW-TECH FAULT FIXING

Connections can work loose, so, without any technical knowledge, you can open the case of PCs and compatibles and make sure that everything appears plugged in tightly. A $45-an-hour technician fixed my faulty disk drive once just by wiggling the lead connected to it.

Last, but by no means least, don't let the ease of writing copy on a word processor carry you away into inordinate length. The technology is great for producing large volumes of copy very quickly, but the media still require releases that are succinct and tightly written.

Audiovisual Media Are Powerful
Even in their simpler forms

Now that video borrowing or renting exceeds the use of library books in the United States, we must accept that we have become a society in which the small-screen recorded image is an increasingly important medium, just as broadcast and cable television became dominant.

Video also can be very inexpensive, now that tape costs have dropped so low—way below the cost of buying and processing film stock. The better amateur hardware produces good quality, duplication is cheap and easy, and playback facilities are universally available.

The inherent interest value of sound and moving visuals can have substantial impact, even if the technical quality is a bit off, whereas similar amateurism in print comes across badly. I experienced this recently when the director of an overseas medical research program, brain research specialist Dr. Mark Gillman, arrived in San Francisco with a tape that had been shot by his teenage sons to show to colleagues and potential sponsors.

OVERCOMING POOR TECHNICAL QUALITY

They did a good job considering the limitations of their equipment and experience, but lack of proper editing facilities and a severe loss of quality because of the transfer from the European PAL system to the US NTSC format detracted substantially from the impact and comprehension of this video, which described a new technique for treating alcohol addiction.

We had only a few hours, no money, and very limited facilities to solve Dr. Gillman's problem before he was due to show the program at the University of California at Berkeley. The solution was quick, inexpensive, and very effective.

As the presentations of the tape were always to be to small groups and Dr. Gillman needed something very portable to carry easily on his travels, I developed a mini–flip chart.

We went through the program together, and I made notes of the key points, particularly the vital statistics of this successful treatment program for alcoholics experiencing withdrawal. The sound track missed some of these and technically was not sufficiently clear for those mentioned to come across with sufficient impact.

GIVING IMPACT TO IMPORTANT POINTS

I keyed important points from the text and the prime statistical information into a personal computer using an ordinary word processing program. The sequence was related directly to the video program and I was careful to put only a few bits of information on each page.

The software program enlarged the type to a size at which it could be read from about 15 feet away, and we ran off the pages on a laser printer. We could have managed with an ordinary, cheaper dot-matrix printer, but the laser printer was available and the printout from it looked very professional.

Using a small easel mounted close to the screen, Dr. Gillman was able to give a whole new dimension to the video, flipping over the pages to the appropriate written information to emphasize what was appearing on the screen at any given time and to convey details that had been left out of the soundtrack.

INTEGRATING VIDEO WITH LIVE PRESENTATIONS

With a remote control on the video recorder, he was able to freeze the program and turn to the flip chart to amplify a point or deal with questions. The video became integrated with a live presentation, it did a much better communication job, and its technical defects were far less apparent. Anyway, he always disarmed his audiences by explaining with pride at the outset that his kids had shot it, good PR showing that his institute used funds for medical research, not elaborate publicity efforts.

For bigger audiences, it is easy to get mini–flip charts generated by personal computer expanded to a larger size. You can do this on a photocopier with enlarging capability, maybe making two or three intermediate enlargements until you reach the size you need and then pasting the pages together to fit on a standard flip chart sheet.

Turning the printout into overhead projector transparencies is easier still. The overhead projector can be a useful supplement to a video program, adding impact and flexibility.

DON'T FORGET THE FLIP CHART

The humble flip chart is often overlooked as technology offers us more sophisticated communications tools. That's a mistake, because it can be powerful and is very closely linked to the presenter to give visual support to the spoken presentation.

Indeed, in one unusual situation it was the only medium for an audiovisual form of presentation. You may find this idea adaptable to PR and training applications in difficult environments.

I was involved with a team trying to persuade the Masai tribesmen in Kenya to stop their nomadic life because their wandering herds of cattle were causing considerable environmental damage. We needed to show them the adverse consequences of their lifestyle, persuade them that settling down and raising crops would bring them positive benefits, and give them basic instruction in simple agricultural techniques.

Showing films or videos was not effective, partly because they were not used to moving, two-dimensional images and were so fascinated by the medium that they lost the message. There would be distractions; for example, film material from overseas used such techniques as jump cuts and close-ups that are familiar in our culture but that were such novelties to many of the Masai tribesmen that they confused and distracted the audience.

Another practical problem was that the presentations needed to be made for the most part without electricity and the budget and other considerations prevented us from using portable generators to power film projectors or video facilities.

CHEAP TO DUPLICATE

Also, with very little money, we had to create a presentation that was easily and cheaply duplicated and self-contained. It had to be set up and used by field workers with limited technical knowledge and communication skills.

The solution was an ordinary, battery-powered cassette recorder and the ubiquitous flip chart. You can record a sound track cheaply—and in different languages, if that is required—and duplicate it quickly and at low cost onto other cassettes. Because only a mono playback is required, the second stero track on the tape can be used to record an electronic beep. In many tape-slide presentations, this beep is used to trigger a change of the projector slide. For the Masai, it could be made audible so that the field worker running the presentation knew when to flip the chart over to the next page to keep up with the audio.

AUTOMATIC PRESENTATION

You don't need to be out in the African bush to use this system, and it can be adapted to a number of PR applications. There are, for example, various display devices that will turn over cards automatically. It is possible to adapt them to run with an audio playback system, perhaps using endless-loop tape to keep the program running automatically.

Whatever method of audiovisual presentation you use, always bear in mind the opportunities and cost of duplicating a program to reach a wider audience. It has always horrified me to see elaborate AVs made at vast expense for special events, when a more effective communication job could be done in a simpler, less-expensive, and more easily duplicated form. Prime examples are those multiprojector, multiscreen presentations, much favored by advertising agencies. They can cost a fortune to produce and then can be shown only on very special occasions—when all the hardware, which usually is operated by very expensive specialists, is assembled.

GO FOR EASY REPETITION

If you must create such a spectacle, at least plan for a simpler version of the same material that will work easily with a single projector and audio playback system. Then you can produce copies with a longer life and the potential to reach a wider audience, not a stack of very expensive projector carousels and tapes that sit on a shelf gathering dust because of the difficulties and expense of showing them.

Video productions are, of course, ideal for repeated screenings in almost any setting in which you can put up a playback machine and a monitor or video projector. Your videotape is easily duplicated and may appeal to a variety of other people who will help to disseminate your message. You also offer the opportunity for others to take extracts and incorporate your material into their own programs.

A good example of this was the *Crashing Cars: Testing for Safety* video made by the Insurance Institute for Highway Safety. It used the video medium very effectively to turn a complex technical subject into dramatic, entertaining and informative material for lay audiences.

TRANSLATING THE TECHNICAL

The institute's communication problem was that most of its work is very technical and for the most part is published in scientific journals. To reach a wider audience, a video was created to show insurers that the institute's work is very relevant to their companies and to explain that their contributions are being spent in the interest of road safety.

A simple documentary approach was adopted because, in this case, the subject matter—crash testing of cars to evaluate how they will behave in an accident—was dramatic enough in itself not to need dressing up. The institute's team showed appropriate restraint as they tightly edited a lot of very interesting footage so that they produced a short and easily digestible program. If only everybody who makes videos or films would exercise similar discipline. The temptation not to cut is indulged too often, and, in this as in any other PR or other communication venture, the audience reactions must always be the prime concern.

PERMIT LIFTING

Sixty major insurers in the United States received copies of the video and many showed it to their employees, while others incorporated it into their own video productions. Never be mean about permitting this "lifting" of your work if it will benefit the dissemination of your message, although it pays to reserve the right to approve the final version to make sure that your message has not been distorted, perhaps unintentionally, by cutting or by unfortunate juxtaposition with other material.

Crash testing reminds me of an episode in which an otherwise very successful PR program backfired badly. I was using a portable rig developed by a crash-test laboratory to simulate the effects of a five-miles-per-hour crash impact. You sat in a car seat wearing a seat belt and were released down a short ramp with an abrupt stop at the bottom. The impact drove home the value of wearing a seat belt and we used the device on a wide scale in all kinds of situations as a corporate image booster and as a public service program to encourage the use of seat belts.

I had my rig all set up outside the Geneva Motor Show and was demonstrating it to a Swedish television crew. As the cameras were whirling, a tiny, elderly, Swiss woman came up and berated me in barely comprehensible French. It seemed that my automotive man-ufacturing client, who sponsored the demonstration, had initiated a minor cost-saving measure—reducing the length of the seat belt web-bing on one model. It didn't affect 99.9 percent of drivers, but this diminutive Swiss woman put her seat so far forward to reach the pedals—and packed in cushions behind and underneath her—that the shortened belt was not long enough to fasten.

The client made a rapid change in specification as a result of this experience. The television crew was sympathetic and did not embar-rass me further by screening the entertaining episode (although the large crowd that had gathered enjoyed a good laugh at my expense).

RATTLING SKELETONS

It taught me a lesson you might benefit from also. In *every* PR venture I undertake, I ask the client to be completely up-front about any aspects of the project or product that might generate negative publicity. Vague replies or evasions are not enough—you must know the potential negatives and tackle them before you get into any publicity or similar communication venture. You don't want any skeletons rattling their way out of the closet to create public or media embarrassment.

There are practical as well as ethical considerations involved and you must make a rational decision on what course to take. Usually it is valid to focus on benefits and plusses and minimize negatives as long as they are not against the public interest. In cases in which there is a real possibility of negative aspects becoming known when media attention is focused on them, then it pays to be open from the beginning and to get them out of the way in as positive a manner as possible, rather than run the risk of being forced later into a defensive position.

Admitting mistakes and offering to compensate for them can be a powerful PR tactic in its own right. It amazed me that there was not a faster, more positive PR effort to deal with that very damaging incident to the American image when an Iranian jetliner, mistaken for a hostile aircraft, was shot down in the Middle East. The error was admitted with commendable speed, but the explanations initially came across as confusing, lame excuses. There could have been an immediate declaration of the intention to compensate families of the victims; instead, the initiative for that gesture passed to demands from anti-American interests.

THE MEDIA NEVER SLEEP

The negative PR was aggravated because the incident occurred on the July 4 weekend and the impression was given internationally that those with responsibilities related to the incident were off enjoying themselves despite the tragedy. There is considerable PR benefit to be accrued by being active while everybody else is on holiday; this activity can boost an image of responsibility and service that can be beneficial to commercial companies as well as to governments. Remember that the media never sleep—or seem to take holidays when you do.

I always make a point of giving my home telephone number to key media people and advise my clients that they should have spokespeople who can be reached 24 hours a day, 365 days a year. If the usual spokesperson is off fishing, then there should be a reserve lined up with call forwarding organized. The call-forwarding facility offered by the telephone companies is a great communications tool.

COMPUTER ANIMATION

Before we leave video, anyone considering productions in this field should keep abreast of what is happening in computer animation. There is some exciting new software available that can produce really impressive images quickly and at low cost. Even modest word processing and graphics software that will run on a Mac or a PC can generate captions and visuals for use in low-budget video productions.

Your budget may not run to using commercial specialists in this developing field. So, if your cause is worthy or if you are prepared to invest some sponsorship money, the computer programmers at local universities may have sophisticated facilities and be strongly motivated to undertake work for you.

Some of the most creative effort in PR is expended to stretch budgets. We tend to forget that there are institutions around us willing to participate in projects at comparatively little or no cost if they see benefits also.

The Powerful Medium of Music
Cost-effective PR campaigns with a tune are more than sweet "ear candy"

When media plans are drawn up for a PR project, there is one very powerful medium almost always overlooked.

Music is a powerful way of reinforcing a message to certain target groups, particularly the young. Coca-Cola and Pepsi do it successfully in their broad international image-boosting and product-awareness campaigns directed primarily at young people through their most popular medium, contemporary music.

The classic example of all time must be the use of music to boost morale among the Dutch when the Nazis occupied the Netherlands during World War II. Staff of the Orange Radio service broadcasting from Britain into occupied Holland scoured London for records of traditional Dutch tunes. They added new, patriotic lyrics, and the music would be listened to by Dutch people despite the risk of strict punishment from the Germans if they were caught. They would go into the streets, shops and work places after a broadcast, whistling the tunes they had just heard and communicating to their compatriots in a very safe but effective way that they had listened to the Dutch free radio and shared the sentiments and messages of hope it had transmitted.

MUSIC CENSORED

The Germans actually censored music in occupied territories as a way of trying to combat resistance, but were never successful. The medium was just too strong for them.

The Orange Radio "020" call sign was painted on walls by Dutch resistance workers to encourage listenership, and, of course, the famous Allied "V for Victory" symbol kept cropping up everywhere. Its Morse code symbol was broadcast in those strong opening notes from Beethoven's Fifth Symphony, which still send a shiver of poignant memories down the spine of anyone who remembers those war years.

This attractive logo was featured on all the PR and other materials produced for the Fort Wayne "Bread 'n Jam" campaign to help the hungry. This is the record and sleeve.

German propaganda minister Goebbels mounted a counter PR campaign to try to make the Allied "V" symbol representative of German victory, but it was a disaster, although his posters were graphically very strong.

WEAK MUSIC IS WEAK PR

I used music as one of the elements of the launch of a new car model called the Capri, commissioning the famous British orchestra leader Sidney Lipton to compose a melody reminiscent of the Mediterranean island of the same name.

It attracted a lot of interest at media presentations and other launch functions, but, on reflection, was not really cost-effective because the tune was not sufficiently strong nor the link forged closely with the product I was promoting.

More success was achieved by the Lincoln National Corporation of Fort Wayne, Indiana; Xerox Learning Systems; the Philadelphia

Water Department; and the City Colleges of Chicago. Promotions of these organizations are among the comparatively few successful exploitations of the medium of music for PR.

Bob Jones, Lincoln National's media relations consultant, recalls how his Indiana community rocked and rolled to feed the hungry—and generated local and national media publicity for a pressing social need in *USA Today,* on the AP wires and the *CBS Evening News* with Dan Rather.

SPARKLING AURAL LANDSCAPE

One of the program's eloquently written media releases sums up the power of music as a communication medium.

"Pop music is more than sweet ear candy. It's a sparkling aural landscape, a familiar echo in your memory, unconsciously whistled or hummed, as potent as it is diverting".

Lincoln National's "Bread 'n Jam" campaign for the hungry latched onto the powerful topical peg of international pop music's activities to support the starving in Ethiopia. It was an intense seven-week series of events to focus attention on the plight of the hungry in the Fort Wayne area and bring them some material benefits.

The campaign climaxed with a midsummer night benefit concert led by singer Nicolette Larson, providing the peg for a multimedia effort that included records, T-shirts, posters, and editorial exposure in the press and on radio and television.

The $28,000 raised directly by the venture was small compared with the immediate and longer-term benefits of public awareness that were generated.

QUANTIFY AWARENESS

"The ripple effect of awareness is immeasurable," commented Father Tom O'Connor of one of the benefitting charities, the St. Mary's Soup Kitchen. Unfortunately, it is very difficult to quantify awareness, but you should try to do so as much as possible, budgeting for some kind of follow-up survey if funds are available, building in response factor measures, and using other devices to quantify these intangible results. That is good self-PR, useful in generating support for future projects.

One of my big regrets is failing to do this when I ran a campaign to change public attitudes towards a major property development project in England. I bathed in a rosy glow of self-congratulation when a previously hostile local community stood and applauded the architects of the scheme at a public meeting that climaxed my campaign. But I failed to collect the hard facts and figures that I could have used on many subsequent occasions to convince clients of the benefits of the attitude-changing techniques I used.

MAKING NATIONAL CONCEPTS WORK LOCALLY

A particularly strong lesson from the Bread 'n Jam project was how effective it can be to take a national—or international—concept and use it in a local context. The international impact of the "We Are The World" and Live Aid efforts for Ethiopia created a receptive local environment for Bread 'n Jam.

The PR strategy during the seven-week build-up included a minimum of one newsworthy announcement every week, correctly beginning with the unveiling of the campaign logo by the CEO of Lincoln National Life. Right at the outset, the logo and the link to a major corporate sponsor were clearly established.

Other participating charities were brought into each of the major prelaunch events; one incongruous twist was the presentation of the trendy T-shirt—featuring the logo, of course—to the local Catholic Bishop.

USING SPONSORSHIP MONEY EFFECTIVELY

Another lesson from this imaginative campaign was the timely deployment of sponsoring money to buy media time to reinforce the PR efforts at the most appropriate moment. Lincoln National stepped in with public service spots to boost concert ticket sales when they proved sluggish a week before the show was due to open.

The sponsor also helped to turn a problem into an opportunity. The unexpected booking of the pop group Crosby, Stills and Nash for another local show just two nights away from the "Bread 'n Jam" performance depressed ticket sales, but Lincoln National persuaded the group to use their event to support the charity effort.

A news conference was staged that included a taped appeal by Graham Nash asking his fans to bring to his show cans of food to donate to the hungry. If you cannot get a celebrity actually to attend a media event, remember that you can always fall back on a cassette or videotape or, better, a telephone or video link.

Another clever touch to make use of "the competition" was to put Bread 'n Jam flyers in with each ticket to The Crosby, Stills and Nash show. The fans brought two tons of canned goods along with them to donate to the cause.

TIMING IS ALL IMPORTANT

There is a temptation by many publicity people—and particularly by their clients—to hold back material until the big event or launch or announcement actually takes place. It is particularly annoying—and counterproductive—when publications are prepared to give coverage but cannot do so unless they receive material well in advance because of the lead times required for their publishing schedules. If they do give coverage after receiving information at the same time as the faster turnaround newspapers and electronic media, they risk looking very dated. They then may be tempted to dig for different—often negative—angles to exploit so that they overcome the lack of topicality by creating an element of controversy.

It always frustrates me when clients refuse to let me hand out the texts of speeches and presentations to journalists at a media event before these are delivered. The justifications range from the desire to keep the information secret to achieve maximum impact at the time of revelation to fears that the boss will be offended as journalists rustle through the texts and are not fully attentive while the boss is speaking.

PRACTICAL NEEDS OF THE MEDIA

What nonsense. The aim of any such PR exercise is to generate maximum publicity, so the practical needs of the media representatives must be paramount. Few of them write shorthand these days, and the tape recorder is a clumsy method of monitoring a speech, so it is far more effective to let journalists check presentation against the text, marking passages they wish to include in their stories. They may jump ahead immediately to the climax of the presentation, but giving them the notes makes their job easier and their quotes more likely to be accurate and increases the chances of fuller coverage.

I always try to show photographers in advance the release photographs that will be distributed because it makes their jobs easier. They can look for different angles and subjects so that they don't just repeat the release photos.

Back to Bread 'n Jam, which showed intelligent timing by releasing a recording of the main new song to be performed at the concert well in advance of the event. This "Give Them Love" anthem, performed by 40 singers and 17 musicians, was released two weeks before the concert with simultaneous play on nine Fort Wayne radio stations.

Similarly, a music video version was released early to local television stations. The video cleverly interspersed scenes of the recording artists with footage of the hunger-relief agencies.

A significant feature of Bread 'n Jam was the positive and powerful editorial opinion coverage it generated.

"'Bread 'n Jam' is a glowing example of Fort Wayne at its finest," commented the *News-Sentinel*. "Local efforts to meet local needs deserve encouragement and support for practical as well as philosophical reasons."

Another example of the power of music was when Xerox Learning Systems used the music video format commercially to add humor and to emphasize elements of a video-based sales training product. It came as a high-impact surprise at the product launch, receiving a standing ovation from the sales force, who asked for copies they could use in the field.

BRINGING COSTS DOWN

By taking advantage of existing material prepared for the training product, this was not an expensive operation. The out-of-pocket costs for the lyricist, crew, costumes, and final post-production were only $5,500. It is a myth to think that videos must be expensive to be effective. When San Francisco Bay's Anchor Outs, the people living on unauthorized boats, staged a concert to publicize their battle with the local authorities, they shot an amateur video portraying their way of life and showed it in the foyer of the theater.

It was a volunteer effort with lots of technical faults, but the impact and interest were tremendous.

You often can get professionals to donate their time to such efforts and bring production costs down. The City Colleges of Chicago did this very effectively when they produced for only $17,000 an elaborate music video that could have cost around $150,000 as a commercial production. The largest expenditure item was unavoidable—film stock and processing expenses.

This project was "The Can't Read, Can't Write Blues" to publicize a program to help the 600,000 functionally illiterate adults in Chicago. One aim was to ease the stigma of illiteracy. The audio-visual medium was particularly appropriate because it was largely directed at an audience that could not read.

Again, both audio and video versions of the tape were distributed to local broadcasting media to generate air time.

TELEPHONE HOTLINES

The City Colleges of Chicago project is one of many examples of the effectiveness of using a telephone hotline—which should always be a toll-free number for national promotions. It is no problem to obtain an easily memorized number—the colleges used the appropriate 642-READ, and the campaign boosted calls by 75 percent.

The Philadelphia Water Department also used music very effectively to curb the multimillion-gallon water loss resulting from youngsters playing with fire hydrants on hot summer days. They locked into the pop culture of their young target audience by creating public service announcements linked to the rap music that was in vogue at the time.

The Department demonstrated the value of generating media involvement and coverage early rather than developing a campaign in isolation and saving everything for a big bang impact. As I discussed earlier, exploit every opportunity along the way for exposure. Department officials and their agency, Gray & Rogers, visited local television stations and showed them the storyboard and played the music before production even began. Two television stations and The *Philadelphia Daily News* actually covered the subsequent taping to generate valuable advance publicity.

VALUE FOR MONEY

This was a remarkably cost-efficient project. It cost about $30,000 and contributed to $300,000-worth of water savings. Average summer day abuse of fire hydrants fell 51.2 percent.

The figures underline the value that can be obtained from PR. It would have cost $2.97 per thousand to reach the more than 21-million television viewers of just the public service announcements. Additional benefits accrued from editorial television coverage because of the news value of the project, and the actual cost of those televised public service announcements was a mere $0.59 per thousand.

To produce and place commercial radio advertisements would have cost $0.94 per thousand. The Philadelphia venture's radio public service announcements reached over 29-million listeners at a cost of only $0.09 per thousand.

Now there's value for money!

Play a Game for Publicity
Another overlooked medium

There are two human weaknesses that can be exploited legitimately in appropriate PR projects. We love to buy things to play with.

Unfortunately, most clients and marketing managers don't seem to take the creation of games as a serious PR tactic, although they are used regularly for other marketing objectives. When I worked overseas on the launch of the first *Star Trek* movie, I thought it an ideal vehicle for a lively board game, but the client disagreed. I took out a product license anyway, and lost a lot of money.

The game was attractive and generated considerable publicity in its own right. Using space photographs from NASA with stills from the movie to create the board and with playing pieces made by members of a local handicapped group, it was a fun family game. However, I was too busy to market it properly, and the stock remained unsold long after the movie finished its main release, and with it went the impetus of topicality to generate sales.

SELF-LIQUIDATING PUBLICITY TOOLS

Board games as a way of making money are a very speculative business and best left to the experts. That is no reason not to create a game that can be a publicity tool and might sell enough units to at least self-liquidate its costs and possibly show a profit.

An appropriate game can be constructed from visual material already created for other aspects of a PR campaign, or you can purchase a license to customize an existing commercial game. Games using boards or playing cards really become viable only if you can manufacture a volume of the game that is sufficient to amortize production costs and bring the unit price down. They make good premiums for the right products and unusual business gifts for Christmas or some corporate function, such as a significant anniversary, plant opening, or product launch.

An international strategy game would be appropriate for a multinational conglomerate or import/export broker, for example.

You could build a game into a company publication, printing the board on the center spread and having cut-out pieces on other pages. Instead of dice, use a six-sided spinner with a number in each segment. Readers cut it out, stick it on a piece of cardboard, and push a toothpick through the middle. Spin it like a top, and the edge on which it comes to rest is the number the player uses to advance over the board.

A MULTILINGUAL GAME

One attraction for 3M when they had an internal PR project to promote a new employee benefit program in Canada was that a game could work well in two languages, English and French.

The 3M game was part of an interlocking comprehensive communication campaign to provide different levels of information in different ways. They called it "Vital Pursuit" and took advantage of the fact that employees were familiar with how to play "Trivial Pursuit", on which it was based. The active involvement required to play such a game underlined the idea that benefit planning is a vital activity and the project offered lots of opportunities to be creative in high-impact, visual ways.

Games often are used in marketing promotions, if rarely as a PR medium. However, I see that McDonald's, GM and Sears got good editorial mileage from their massive joint promotion involving facsimiles of the Monopoly board, with cards representing Monopoly properties available at McDonald's restaurants. It enabled Sears and GM, who gave prizes, to promote their products to the youngsters who patronize the leading fast food chain.

SPORTING PUBLICITY

Other games—primarily sports games—are also excellent communication tools. I worked once with a talented manufacturing manager who encouraged—and found financial support for—golf and soccer tournaments between his staff and employees from companies that supplied him with components. The good personal relationships established at these events gave him tangible cost-benefits in smoothing out supply problems, especially critical in these days of "just-in-time" manufacturing, when components are delivered to the production line only just before they need to be used.

English and American diplomats—and several companies from these countries operating overseas—have used their national sports of cricket and baseball as excellent PR tools to project a positive image and generate good local relations.

Sports sponsorship is, if you'll pardon the pun, a completely different ball game. You need to be careful about getting involved in sponsoring sporting events and make quite sure that the PR objectives are clearly spelled out and that PR is not being used as a way to plunder budgets and justify participation in an event that is of personal interest to the CEO or a charity, not a viable PR activity in its own right.

Large sums are spent each year sponsoring individual holes in golf tournaments and rarely do I see them justifying their costs.

If any reader has a lot of money and shares my enthusiasm for board games, I've got one or two up my sleeve just waiting for a backer. One is an investment game, similar in some respects to Monopoly, that could be used as the medium for presenting annual report results. Shareholders use the same rules and parameters within which the company had to operate during the year and see if they can do better.

That is an idea starter. Other games could be created to familiarize employees with a company's group or global operations; with the way a product is designed, developed and brought to market; or to illustrate the financial impact of excessive union demands for salary and benefit increases.

The scope is almost limitless. Over to you!

(P.S.: Don't forget the capacity of various computer software programs—including desktop publishing ones—to handle much of the difficult work in designing and creating artwork for a board or card game.)

Compiling the Media Kit
Blimps are the medium and *the message*

The biggest, longest-running, most familiar promotional objects in the history of the PR business are the Goodyear airships, so I am using them as an example for a practical, comprehensive media kit.

When a blimp goes out on an assignment likely to generate media coverage, comprehensive media kits are available to help journalists with background information and generate positive media coverage. On these pages you will find the typical elements of such a kit which demonstrate how this PR activity should be handled.

THE FOLDER

Media releases, photographs and background information all go in the stiff cardboard folder, which costs comparatively little to produce, is eye-catching, and goes in a standard mailing envelope to offer enough protection to keep the contents crisp and undamaged.

It is printed in the Goodyear corporate blue—just one color on white cardboard stock, which keeps the cost way down and looks far more expensive than it actually is. The folder is timeless, simple, impressive and functional.

There are two flaps on the inside, one on each of the facing pages. They are manufactured using standard die cuts and folds, there are no expensive special printing setups required and reordering is easy.

There are two parallel folds down the center, not just the one often found. This way, the flaps can be loaded with a considerable amount of documentation and the folder will still close flat, like a bound book. There is a slit in the flaps so that business cards can be inserted and not get misplaced.

THE GOODYEAR TIRE & RUBBER COMPANY - Akron, Ohio 44316

A simple, but impressive, folder for the media kit.

THE VISUALS

Goodyear sent the kit to me in the normal way, with two black-and-white, full-plate-size photographs, one showing the airship Columbia on the ground, the other in flight. In one photograph it is pointing to the right and in the other to the left. I have a choice, which could be quite crucial in designing the page on which the pictures are to be used.

A choice of photographs focusing right and left helps editors to design pages.

Line drawings are economical, flexible visuals.

Positioning visuals is a key element of graphic design. If the layout had forced me to put the picture of the airship in the top left-hand corner of a left-hand page or on a front page, I would be cursing Goodyear if they had sent only a shot of the blimp pointing to the left. It would appear to fly out of the page, taking the reader's eye with it. I write a lot about transport, and it is really infuriating to get a media kit on a new truck, car, plane, or motorcycle in which the product faces the same direction in all the photographs, which often are shot from much the same angle. Such sloppiness limits picture editors' choice and may be the difference between only one instead of two or more pictures being used.

THE CAPTIONS

Each caption is printed on a single sheet of paper, which is folded and perforated to form two sections. The actual text of the caption will tear away from the picture easily, so that it can be edited and sent off for setting. The other section remains stuck to the picture, cross-referenced to the caption by means of the first words. The logo and the contact address are printed on both sections, simply and cleanly preprinted in the single corporate color.

The text for each caption is short and informative and contains just enough background information to be complete in itself. It is printed in large clear typewriter type, with double-spaced lines and wide margins all around the text to facilitate editing.

A plain white paper stock is used for the captions and is preferable for readability and appearance. There is no need for fancy tints. The Goodyear library reference number is stamped lightly on the back of the actual photo print and will not interfere with any scaling or cropping marks a picture editor may need to make.

A third visual—a cartoon drawing—is included also. It will reproduce easily, even on the worst paper and printer, and is simple and clean so that it can be reduced in size. It could be used in a variety of ways, perhaps run very small in a single column.

MEDIA RELEASES

There are five separate and completely self-contained media releases. Each one can be run as sent to coincide with the visit of the *Columbia* to a local newspaper's area or customized with a new introductory paragraph or two. They also can be blended easily together for one composite news story or feature.

They give a selection of angles and can be adapted readily to almost any publishing situation or for use in a radio or television story or news item. Each is timeless, includes lots of facts and focuses on the airship, with a comparatively soft sell of the Goodyear connection. Lengths vary from a single page to a seven-page feature article with the sheets single-stapled in the top left corner so that they can be separated with a quick flick of the wrist. Each page should carry a slug or keyword to identify to which story it belongs, in case the pages get mixed up.

No paragraphs should run over from one page to another. The text should not be crammed too tightly; use double spacing and wide margins all around to leave plenty of room for editing marks.

AIRSHIPS

To millions of Americans, the word "blimp" means just one thing— Goodyear. For more than 60 years, the Goodyear airships have been performing yeoman service. The graceful lighter-than-air craft log nearly 200,000 air miles each year in their travels across the United States and Europe.

Since 1917, Goodyear has built more than 300 lighter-than-air craft, more than any other company in the world. Of that number, 60 have been commercial airships, which Goodyear has used as "Aerial Ambassadors."

The remaining airships were constructed under contract for the Army and Navy.

The Army withdrew from lighter-than-air operations in the 1930s. The Navy phased out its airships in 1962, leaving the skies to the Goodyear fleet of the America, Columbia, Enterprise and Europa.

AIRSHIP CLASSIFICATIONS

Rigid airships, such as the Goodyear-built Akron and Macon, had metal frameworks within their envelopes to maintain their shape.

In semi-rigid construction, the airship had a rigid or jointed keel that ran the length of the envelope. This keel and the pressure of the lifting gas gave the envelope its shape.

In non-rigid models, such as the Enterprise, Columbia, America and Europa, the envelope shape is maintained entirely by the internal pressure of the helium gas aided by air cells, or ballonets, to compensate for pressure differences. There is no internal framework.

It is equally correct to refer to a blimp as a dirigible, for by definition a dirigible is a "lighter-than-air" craft that is engine-driven and steerable. Only a rigid airship is a Zeppelin.

WHY A BLIMP IS A BLIMP

The most plausible explanation, the experts now claim, is that the term "blimp" originated with Lt. (later Air Commodore) A. D. Cunningham of the Royal Navy Air Service, who, in December of 1915, commanded the air station at Capel.

As the story goes, Cunningham was conducting a weekly inspection tour of the station. While inspecting His Majesty's Airship SS-12, he playfully reached up and flipped his thumb at the gasbag. An odd noise echoed off the taut fabric.

Cunningham smiled, then orally imitated the sound his thumb had drummed out of the airship bag: "BLIMP!" The rest is history.

SKILLED PERSONNEL AND SPECIAL EQUIPMENT

A team of qualified specialists, supported by equipment especially designed for lighter-than-air activities, makes possible the efficiency of Goodyear Airship Operations.

As special representatives of the world's largest rubber company, personnel associated with the operation are selected not only for their professional skill, but for their outstanding character as well.

Each ship is staffed by five pilots, 16 ground crewmen and a public relations representative.

The pilot-in-charge of each airship is responsible for the crew and equipment. Based on weather conditions and other circumstances, the decision to fly on any given day is the responsibility of the pilot-in-charge.

Pilots complete a comprehensive Goodyear lighter-than-air training program before receiving FAA pilot certification.

Ground crewmen play dual roles. In addition to handling the airship during takeoffs, landings and moorings, they also serve as licensed radio technicians, mechanics, riggers, electricians, night sign specialists and clerks.

Equipment includes a ground crew bus, a large tractor-trailer rig and a van.

In addition to transporting the crew, the bus serves as office headquarters. The van is used as a command car and utility vehicle.

The tractor unit is a mobile maintenance facility. It also carries the portable mooring mast.

The airship and all vehicles are linked by two-way radio communication.

RIDE INFORMATION

Goodyear wishes it could accommodate everyone who would like to ride in the blimp.

This, however, is physically impossible because the America, Columbia, Enterprise and Europa can carry only a few passengers in each of the many cities they visit every year. The maximum passenger capacity of each ship is just six persons per flight.

Because of the heavy demand for flights when the airships conduct their summer tours (May through October), we are limited to conducting rides for members of the press, radio and television, and special guests of Goodyear by invitation only.

Front page of the brochure—it could easily have been produced by desktop publishing.

AN AIRSHIP FOR EUROPE

A Goodyear airship — a sister to the lighter-than-air craft that are a familiar sight to millions of Americans — is now plying the skies of Europe and England.

The airship, christened Europa, tours the Continent annually during the spring and summer, following schedules similar to her American sister ships Enterprise, Columbia and America.

During the winter months, Europa operates from a 52½-million home base at Cedena, Italy, just 18 miles north of Rome.

The Europa is a frequent visitor at sports events, auto races and air shows, and a staunch supporter in helping celebrate and promote community activities and civic projects. Her activities continue the public service and public relations traditions established in more than her 60 years of Goodyear airship operations in the United States.

Components of the airship were constructed at Goodyear facilities in Akron, Ohio and Litchfield Park, Arizona.

The completed subassemblies were airlifted to the Royal Aircraft Establishment's historic airship hangars at Cardington, England. The Europa was erected and test-flown there before making her first English Channel crossing and European tour in 1972.

NAMES ARE A TRADITION ...

In the early days of Goodyear's activity in lighter-than-air, the late P.W. Litchfield, chief executive of the company, envisioned the blimp as an aerial yacht.

As a result, all of Goodyear's domestic commercial airships have been named after yachts that have won the famed America's Cup Race. The Enterprise was named for the 1930 victor. Yachts christened Columbia were victorious in 1871, 1899, 1901 and 1958. America's namesake won the very first America's Cup Race back in 1851.

... and so is safety

Goodyear is proud of its airship safety record. In more than 60 years of commercial operations carrying passengers, more than 1,000,000 men, women and children have flown in our airships without an injury.

AIRSHIPS RIVAL STARS WITH NIGHT SIGNS

All four airships of the Goodyear fleet are equipped with incandescent night signs to flash after-dark messages from the sky.

The "Super Skytacular" signs on each of the blimps are 105 feet long and 24.5 feet high. Each includes 3,780 lamps, or a total of 7,560 per ship.

Messages to be run on the sign are born on exotic electronic equipment in a special lab in Akron. A technician "draws" the animation and copy on a cathode ray tube with a light gun. From there a computer takes over.

A typical six-minute show consists of 40 million pieces or bits of "on-off" information which, when run through special electronic readers aboard the airship, control lamp and color selection.

Through the wonders of "Super Skytacular," Santa's sleigh and reindeer flash across the Yuletide skies ... a turkey narrowly escapes becoming a Thanksgiving dinner ... a giant firecracker explodes to form an American flag ... and many others, including special animations flown by Europe to commemorate European holidays and activities.

Approximately 75 percent of the messages run on the night signs of the Goodyear airship are devoted to public service projects in behalf of non-profit charities and service organizations.

AN EYE FOR SPORTS

Blimps and sporting events have become virtually synonymous. From the Rose Bowl to the Indy 500, blimps provide superb aerial platforms for TV viewers.

A specially modified, Goodyear-supplied, light weight color camera and on-board electronics are used for the telecasts. A microwave transmitter sends the camera signals to the ground where a dish antenna picks them up.

A network cameraman and video technician are on board the blimp. A third network crewman on the ground keeps the dish antenna positioned skyward to receive the signals from the blimp. The pilot listens for cues to position the airship.

It is this teamwork between the network and Goodyear blimp personnel that provides fans with spectacular blimp-eye views of the sporting event.

COMPONENTS OF AN AIRSHIP

1. Nose Cone Battens (supports)
2. Forward Ballonet (air bag inside envelope)
3. Catenary Curtain and (inside envelope)
4. Aft Ballonet
5. Control Surfaces (rudders and elevators)
6. Car—Passenger Compartment
7. Engines
8. Night Sign Lamps
9. Air Scoops (channel air to ballonets)
10. Air Valves (regulate air in ballonet)
11. Helium Valve

VITAL STATISTICS

Overall Dimensions:		
Length	192 feet	
Height	59 feet	
Width	50 feet	
Volume	202,700 cubic feet	

Power:		
Twin Continental Engines (6 cylinders, pusher type)	210 hp. each	
Cruising Speed	35 mph.	
Maximum Speed	50 mph.	

Weight and Lift:		
Maximum Gross Weight	12,320 lbs.	
Weight Empty	9,500 lbs.	
Maximum Lift	2,820 lbs.	
No. of Passengers	Six plus pilot	

Operational Limits:		
Normal Altitude	1,000-3,000 feet	
Maximum Altitude	10,000 feet	
Range	500 miles	

Envelope Fabric:		
Material (2-ply)	Rubber-coated Polyester Fabric	
Night Sign:	"Super Skytacular"	
Number of lights	7,560 total (both sides)	
Height of Sign	24.5 feet	
Length of Sign	105 feet	
Amount of Wiring	80 miles	
Readability	1 mile	
Colors	Red, Green, Blue, Yellow	

1. **Overhead Control Panel:** Contains controls for communications, fuel and electrical systems.
2. **Throttles and Propeller Pitch Controls:** Throttles regulate speed of engines. Pitch controls regulate angle at which propeller blades "bite" the air. Propellers are constant speed and reversible.
3. **Mixture and Heat Controls:** Regulate the degree to which fuel is mixed with air in the engine and control the temperature of the fuel-air mixture to prevent icing.
4. **Envelope Pressure Controls:** These regulate helium and ballonet air pressure to maintain the trim and shape of the airship envelope.
5. **Flight Instrument Panel:** Contains (from left to right) flight, navigation and engine indicator instruments.
6. **Rudder Pedals:** Regulate airship's right and left direction.
7. **Elevator Wheel:** Controls airship's up and down direction.

Such a fact-filled brochure is well worth including in a media kit.

Another release has a selection of brief items, useful as fillers when making up a page or for panels or other text breakers. It comes with a clear summary of physical details of the Columbia that could drop straight into a panel on the page.

THE BROCHURE

The kit is completed by a low-cost, two-color (black text and the corporate blue for headings) brochure with more vital statistics and comprehensive information. If you have an attractive brochure, include it with media kits to give more substance to them and to provide a quick reference.

That's it. Simple, functional, and very practical for media people of all kinds to use. No gimmicks, and none needed. Would that all media kits followed such a format!

Scrounging to Cut Costs
The PR material is usually there, if you only ask for it

Rarely when you undertake a PR project does there seem to be enough in the budget to achieve all your objectives. My first step is always to search around for what I can scrounge for nothing.

First stops are the marketing, training, manufacturing, and research departments; there I look for visuals of all kinds to use in my media kits and on posters and other materials. This essential first step occurs before I attempt to hire graphic artists and photographers. If these departments do not have anything in the way of graphics or photographs that I can use, then often we can do a deal to share production costs.

Even if a photographic shoot planned by the marketing or training people was not intended originally to generate material that would be applicable to PR needs, it is a lot less expensive to ride on the back of the other department's project. If the props, lighting, models and other paraphernalia are all being set up to do a television commercial, sales brochures, or training films and manuals, then I arrange either to keep the photographer for an extra hour or two to shoot what I need or to have my own photographer around.

THE SHAMPOO SCAM

On one occasion I locked into the marketing department's production of a TV commercial for a new brand of shampoo, which, the sales material proclaimed, had been developed in the laboratories by a venerable French expert in hair care.

It seemed a great opportunity to develop media material, until investigation revealed that the French expert didn't exist. He was a complete figment of the advertising agency's imagination. They might get away with it—in fact, they did—but there was no way outright deception like that could be justified for the PR campaign.

However, I turned up with my Hasselblad for the TV commercial shoot. I got good pictures suitable for various media releases and

Visuals like this may be created by other departments and either used as is or adapted for release to the media, without plundering the PR budget.

an excellent women's magazine picture-story featuring the model being used in the commercial, which plugged the new shampoo very effectively. Generating a feature like that and all those photographs as a separate PR exercise would have cost thousands, but, by riding on the back of the marketing activities, the only expenses were my time and a few rolls of film.

"FREE" VISUALS

The illustration of the "typical" woman car buyer that featured in a General Motors media kit is an excellent example of how a sales department project was turned into editorial material.

Chevrolet introduced a sales training program designed to help salespeople learn how to improve their approach to young people and women, who are assuming much greater importance in car- and truck-buying decisions. The program recognized that female and younger buyers have needs that are different from those of traditional male automobile customers. This graphic was produced to illustrate the profiles of typical women customers.

An attractive brochure aimed at potential women buyers had been produced for free distribution by Chevrolet dealers, and, with a couple of media releases and a reproducible halftone photograph of the graphic, made an attractive editorial kit.

OVERCOMING NEGATIVE ATTITUDES

Digging for free material should be coupled with the investigating and listening process that lies at the heart of good PR programs. Be prepared for negative attitudes at first, particularly among researchers and engineers, until they get to know and trust you and understand your PR needs.

On several occasions, I have gone from a "hyped-up", enthusiastic briefing on a new car or truck model to dig among the engineers for product developments of real editorial substance, only to find a far more negative attitude among these specialists.

"Well, there's nothing really exciting for you," they would say. "The styling changes look good, but there's not much new or interesting under the skin."

PROBE FOR THE DETAILS

Then, you start chatting, probing for details that might be useful. I find the best results come from getting a group of development engineers together so that a friendly competition is generated among them, and they push their own detail projects.

In the case of one face-lifted car model—not a Chevrolet—such a session began with expressions of disappointment that some of the more interesting developments on which the engineers were working had not been put into production yet. However, one engineer had devoted a lot of time to developing the use of a new material for suspension components which did feature in the facelift. The main benefit was that the components were cheaper to manufacture, but there were also improvements in maintenance and road holding.

We conveniently forgot the manufacturing-cost savings in our PR material, and we played up the maintenance and road-holding benefits for the customer. Indeed, I built a whole campaign, which worked throughout Europe and in a number of other sales territories, around the road-holding improvements.

I scrounged from the engineers impressive-looking technical drawings for the media kit and got their free help in developing two promotional products. One was a modern version of the flicker books which used to be popular in the early days of photography. You take a sequence of pictures like the frames in a strip of movie film but with the action developing far more rapidly. Then you reproduce those pictures in a small, pocket-book form. When the pages are flicked with the thumb, the individual pictures blend to create a semblance of movement.

We borrowed a special sequence camera from a newspaper friend—never hire or buy when you can borrow!—and one of the engineers drove the car around one of the most famous racing corners in European motor racing—at the Brands Hatch circuit near London. The resulting flicker book was widely distributed and added impact to the media kit. It gave much more substance to the handling improvements, which were very subjective anyway, and helped us to "sell" the benefits of this feature editorially.

GET "FREE" EXPERT TIME AS WELL

The engineers also helped to develop a very simple, low-cost device which we used as part of a series of demonstrations and competitions by dealers throughout Europe. It was a molded plastic dish containing a heavy ball fastened to the hood of the car. The competition involved maneuvering the car on a twisty route around pylons while keeping the ball in the dish.

The message was that the new car had such superior road-holding capability that you could maneuver quite violently without dislodging the ball. In fact, you could have achieved similar results with the old model and most of the competition's products, but the perception was that our car was superior.

If I had tried to put that program together independently, it would have been very expensive. Stimulating the enthusiasm of the engineering department enabled me to get many expensive hours of expertise and cooperation that didn't cost a penny.

Indeed, the ball in the bowl gimmick was so successful for PR that the marketing department picked it up, giving me a lever for future favors from them!

MOTIVATE YOUR EXPERTS

Too many PR people think that researchers and engineers are stodgy, unimaginative types preoccupied with their technology and not much good for publicity purposes. I have found the opposite to be true, after you have motivated them and turned them into powerful allies for imaginative PR activities. If you try to get them involved in projects with more hype than substance, though, they are turned off just as quickly.

They also become reluctant to cooperate if you overwhelm them with time-consuming PR activities that intrude too much into their main work.

The brilliant PR people at Daimler-Benz made effective use of the driving simulator that the engineering team at the company's West Berlin facility had developed.

I was among the hordes of journalists who flew in to Berlin from all over the world to undergo the remarkable experience of "driving"

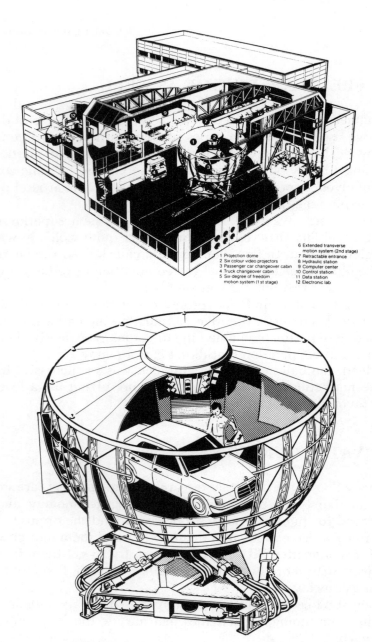

1 Projection dome
2 Six colour video projectors
3 Passenger car changeover cabin
4 Truck changeover cabin
5 Six-degree of freedom
  motion system (1st stage)

6 Extended transverse
  motion system (2nd stage)
7 Retractable entrance
8 Hydraulic station
9 Computer center
10 Control station
11 Data station
12 Electronic lab

Cut-away three-dimensional diagrams are useful supplementary visual material for PR activities. Daimler-Benz produced these for its driving simulator in Berlin, which generated enormous international publicity. Often such drawings can be obtained at no additional cost from the training, engineering, or marketing department. They reproduce best if distributed as glossy photographic prints, but you may get away with good quality photocopies if the artwork is clear.

188

a car inside the simulator, with computers generating all kinds of road and weather conditions and the car responding exactly as it would in real life.

The amount of publicity that device has generated worldwide to boost the image of Daimler-Benz for advanced quality engineering has been remarkable, but the PR people had to ease off in their use of this exceptional promotional device to allow the engineers more time for their research.

While that is an exceptional situation, there are lots of fascinating things going on in R&D, manufacturing and product-testing facilities that PR people fail to exploit, and so miss valuable opportunities to boost their company's or their clients' products and images.

Exploiting Technology—with a Dash of Human Interest

An important lesson in effective internal and external PR

Poor General Motors is receiving a bashing from the media these days, but the giant corporation's PR people provide a number of lessons on how to handle both aggressive and defensive public relations efficiently.

The interlocking global campaigns for Magnequench and the Sunraycer solar car are outstanding examples from which we all can learn, with results in positive media coverage demonstrating the remarkable cost-efficiency that can be achieved when skilled communications people get their hands on highly promotable projects.

The Magnequench program, led by Delco Remy's Director of Public Relations, Keith J. Pitcher, is particularly interesting in the way that it has projected a highly complex and not very easily visualized technological development. Although the scale of this venture is vast, the principle of the PR techniques used can be applied to the publicizing of technology in a wide variety of situations and can work just as well on a more limited scale.

Magnequench is a revolutionary invention in magnetics that could come to rank along with the microchip as one of the most significant inventions of recent decades. A stream of molten metal is cooled—quenched—instantly when it contacts a spinning wheel in an oxygen-free environment. This rapid solidification creates magnetic metallic ribbon-flakes, which are further processed to produce magnets that are up to ten times more powerful than conventional ferrite magnets. The main benefit is that the size and weight of electric motors can be reduced dramatically.

The applications range from motor vehicles to children's toys, microwave ovens to furnaces, computers to mass transport systems, and high-tech medical diagnosis to vacuum cleaners and refrigerators.

This picture of Ann Marie Reilly of Detroit—always use the model's name to add human interest, even if he or she is a professional and not an employee—tells the story succinctly in one shot. She holds a familiar object, a vacuum cleaner, which typifies the consumer benefits of the new technology. On the table in front of her are flakes of the new magnetic ribbon. Next to them are examples of the magnets into which the flakes can be formed. The composition of the picture has added attraction to a publication because it can so easily be turned into a cutout. A deep etch around the outline of Ann Marie, the right edge of the vacuum cleaner, and the table top separates the subject matter from the background, and you have a powerful image to put at the top left of a page with the heading running alongside to the right.

She is looking straight out of the picture in an engaging, friendly way which adds to the impact. The picture is accompanied by an extended, but still tightly written and easily comprehended, caption, which is attached to the back of the print with a short length of clear tape and removed easily. This is a much better alternative than glue, which can both tear the paper of the caption and damage the back of the print as an editor tries to separate the two.

Here we have a clear, simple illustration of the *benefits* of the new technology and a tie-in to the product and brand names. The cranking motor on the left is supplied by Delco Remy for Chevrolet and GMC pickup trucks and is half the size and weight of the conventional cranking motor on the right.

STRONG VISUALS ARE INVALUABLE

Keith Pitcher's team has been exploiting this technological break-through in some very powerful PR efforts in recent years to benefit both the corporate image and individual products. Particularly interesting is the range of visuals they have used, some of which are reproduced here. They overcome many of the problems of making very complex technology—especially something as difficult to illustrate as magnetism—both comprehensible and interesting to lay audiences.

GM milked this venture for PR opportunities worldwide before it took place, during the event and afterwards. It was a major internal PR effort to praise and motivate employees as well as a powerful, external image–building program. It projected a much-needed new image of innovation and technological prowess.

I particularly liked the way that the people involved in the project were the focus of much of the media material disseminated. It is a tactic that works well in the general media and benefits internal PR efforts also.

The message is reinforced by distributing pictures of the vehicles in which the new technology is used, creating opportunities for media exposure of the product the public can actually buy.

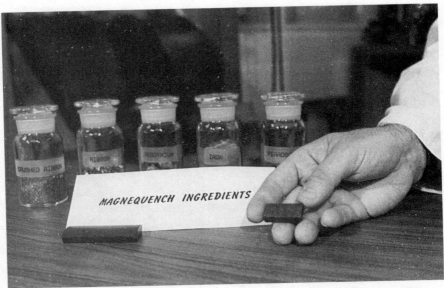

Here is a good close-up of the Magnequench ingredients. It is not very imaginative, but it tells the story and may be useful to editors as a small supplementary picture that can be used almost anywhere in a layout, even in a single column if a story turns to a page dominated by advertising and an illustration is needed to help the editorial compete for reader attention.

magnequench

Production Capability
PROCESS COMPARISON

MQIII   SINTERED

| ALLOY |
| RAPID SOLIDIFICA-TION |
| HOT FORM |
| MAGNETIZE |

| ALLOY |
| CRUSH |
| GRIND |
| BLEND |

| ALIGN & PRESS |
| SINTER |
| FINISH GRIND |
| MAGNETIZE |

This line drawing can also be reduced and still convey a clear technical explanation of the manufacturing process.

GENERAL MOTORS CORPORATION
"World's Largest User of Automotive Magnets"

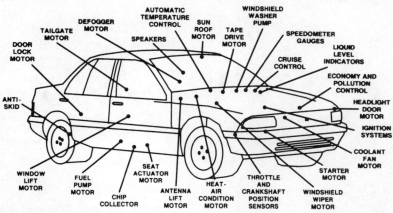

Another line drawing conveys graphically all the many automotive applications of the new technology. The corporate plug at the top is well away from the visual and can be eliminated. Most publications will prefer to eliminate it.

magnequench

Key Technology
RAPID SOLIDIFICATION

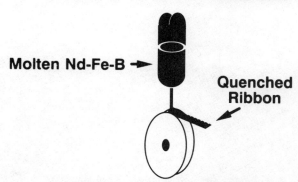

Molten Nd-Fe-B →

Quenched
Ribbon

• Quench Rate ~ 1,000,000°C/sec

Technical publications love diagrams. This is a clear one that many of them have published in their coverage of Magnequench. Diagrams, bar charts, graphs, and the like are quick, easy, and economical to produce these days with readily available computer software. There is no excuse for not including them with media releases, if appropriate.

Don't forget the people! Even the highest tech PR material should still include human interest items. In this case, Delco Remy shows a group of employees to reflect their new management system, in which the accent is on employee participation.

Don't hestitate to include a shot of a facility as a "scene-setter" for editorial material about new products and processes. However, both this and the employee group could have been made visually more interesting. With both external and internal pictures of facilities, I always try to get people prominently in the shot to add human interest.

The Magnequench PR effort was given further impetus when the technology was used in GM's Sunraycer car, which won the inaugural transcontinental World Solar Challenge race in Australia by more than 600 miles.

EXTERNAL PR ACHIEVING INTERNAL OBJECTIVES

In the release announcing the victory, the first quote was chairman Roger Smith speaking about "your triumph of teamwork", and the whole theme is about pride in a successful team effort. Much of the emphasis in all the PR material is on the coming together of 16 different GM organizations and suppliers on four continents.

Many of the GM releases were comprehensive, detailing the other competitors, and the 1,950-mile route and giving other data that made the automaker's press kit a convenient ready-reference tool for journalists. Your own message stands a much better chance of being used when you package in this way all the facts a journalist needs. Even when you are only one of many commercial interests participating in a major event such as this, the quality and comprehensiveness of your release material can make you an authoritative

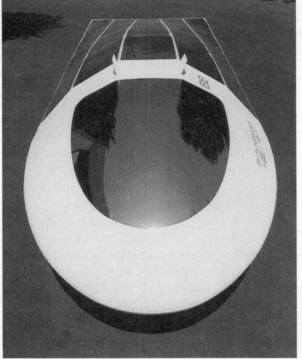

Compare these two shots of the Sunraycer used so successfully as a major international PR vehicle. The one in which there is a human figure has far more visual interest, and there is also a better indication of scale.

source, used perhaps even more by the press than are the media services offered by the official organizers.

ENLIGHTENED LONG-TERM APPROACH

There are numerous examples of this enlightened approach to PR. British Oil and Cake Mills, a major animal feed supplier, would have a special center for journalists at all the big agricultural shows in Britain. Often you would find more journalists working there and using it as a base than they did the show organizers' press tent—and not just because of the plentiful supply of liquid refreshment! The company's PR people made it a hub of activity and information, building up long-term relationships with the media. Their emphasis was on serving journalists' needs rather than on seeking short-term benefits from editorial mentions.

Such an enlightened approach enables you to become an established source of comprehensive information about your industry or sphere of activity. I was retained for a long time by Toyota in South Africa to analyze the monthly returns on national vehicle sales and to produce a comprehensive briefing that was authoritative and fair to the industry as a whole and that helped media people to interpret what was going on.

Many journalists would wait for our story rather than run with the official industry release and figures simply because we provided a good service. Management soon recognized the long-term value of being in this position, and our monthly release often would contain information that was not always in the client's interests to publicize but that was essential to maintain the perception of the client as an authoritative source.

UNIQUE LOGOSTYLES

All the media releases GM generated for the Sunraycer project had a special heading with a unique logostyle and, beneath it, the logos of the main subsidiaries involved. It makes good sense to create a unique logostyle for media material for a special project or event, as long as the corporate identification is still prominent.

Of course, there is always the risk of not winning contests of this kind, and the aim should be to get a high proportion of your PR returns up front, so that victory, if it comes, is the cherry on the top. Sometimes a valiant loser can grab the headlines away from the winners.

An example of this occurred when I covered the Monte Carlo Rally for a number of publications and radio stations. The British Motor Corporation's team of Minis was denied victory by the French officials' interpretation of the rules. This caused a furor that got the British more positive coverage than the French winners received. It was a freak situation, but the BMC people made the most of it by continuing their excellent PR, which included ready accessibility to team officials and crews for interviews, despite their disappointment and frustration.

In that same rally, one of the Japanese cars caught fire, and I must admit, as a journalist, to aggravating the negative PR generated for the manufacturer by that incident. When I interviewed the driver and navigator afterwards, they said that when their fire extinguishers failed to put out the flames they tried urinating on the burning engine, as no other liquids were available. It made a popular story that generated a lot of unsought publicity because of its amusing human interest angle.

COPING UNDER PRESSURE

When considering sponsorships or the selection of personnel for events, carefully examine their ability to cope with the media under pressure. The competitor, manager, or support crew, who are excessively dedicated to winning without regard for PR considerations could be a bad investment for your sponsorship dollar, especially if they are poor losers and show it.

The Scandinavian rally driver Rauno Aaltonen showed how it should be done in that same Monte Carlo rally. He was moving very quickly when his Mini lost a wheel during one of the special stages. The incident put him farther back down the field. He—and the car—got very positive coverage for this mishap after he told me that he had continued with one of the special stages on only three wheels and still managed to finish.

The final PR word on the Sunraycer has not yet been written, because it continues to be used for promotions, including that most valuable spin-off of any successful PR campaign—generating potential buyer traffic through retail outlets. With any motor industry promotion, I always look for ways in which we can make it benefit the dealers by generating extra showroom traffic. That should be a universal principle, much easier to achieve when PR in a company is closely linked to the marketing department and is not made a responsibility, as it sometimes is, of some other department, such as personnel.

I've never been able to quantify it, but I suspect that there is a much higher incidence of ineffective PR when it is a function executed apart from the corporate communicators who are concentrated in the marketing area. Even many in-house journals produced within the human resources area could benefit if they were to become the responsibility of the marketing department; they then would be approached professionally as *internal* marketing activities.

I once had to take over a company newspaper that was not coming out regularly, and had boring content, and lacked credibility because production was being handled by the personnel department. With the best of intentions, they just did not understand the communication business.

Another practical plus of making internal PR part of a company's marketing efforts is that much of the cost can ride on the back of marketing budgets and you can get economical input from the advertising agency and market research. The advertising specialists must not dictate the PR tactics, as they are distinctly different disciplines.

Don't Forget Radio and Audio Tapes
The great one-to-one medium

We live in a very visual world in which pictures and written words are regarded as the most powerful communication media.

However, there are two very contrasting examples of the continuing impact of purely aural PR activities.

Radio is still a tremendous medium, as agricultural equipment manufacturer Case IH demonstrated in its farm radio broadcasting project. It is even possible to exploit the boom in portable audio cassette players, such as the Sony Walkman, or those installed in vehicles, as university students in China showed very effectively.

The Case IH people cost-efficiently got into direct contact with the prime radio media people by hosting an interview suite when 170 of these broadcasters gathered in Kansas City for the annual National Association of Farm Broadcasters' convention. However scattered your target audience, there usually is at least one occasion each year on which many of them get together, providing you with an easy and efficient way to reach them.

There were always at least two of the company's representatives in the suite to give interviews. The broadcasters were alerted to this facility by posters around the convention hotel and by cards distributed as delegates registered.

SPECIAL RADIO KITS

The media people received a specially tailored radio kit that included prerecorded cassettes—accompanied by written transcripts—on topical subjects of interest to their audiences. It was a very soft sell, with Case IH mentioned only to identify the company experts featured on the tapes.

Special effort was made to make the tapes of maximum use to the differing needs of each broadcaster.

The interviews were available in two formats, one with a professional broadcaster asking the questions, and the other in open-ended versions, from which the interviewer's words had been erased. The broadcasters could insert their own lead-ins and questions into the resulting dead air spaces. The movie industry uses these open-ended interviews with showbiz personalities in both audio and video form to generate valuable airtime, but PR practitioners in other industries often overlook this effective tool.

The Case IH effort at the convention reached over 560,000 farm households in all the major agricultural regions of the United States, and there was effective follow-up to make good use of the radio media contacts made at the convention.

CHINESE MAKE AUDIO WALL POSTERS

One example of imaginative use of audio created a new medium. Wall posters have been a traditional medium for expressing dissent in many countries, but they are vulnerable to action by the authorities. University students in Peking found it very frustrating that they would put posters up one day and find them torn down by the next.

They started gathering at night, recording into portable cassette machines the messages on wall posters, and then duplicating the tapes onto other cassettes to be distributed widely for playback on personal tape players. Soon the new medium became very popular, especially the more entertaining tapes narrated by attractive voices.

In mainland China, this was a practical, low-cost approach using a new medium in an imaginative new way. Over in more affluent Taiwan, opposition groups used video recordings to spread their message, a technique that proved particularly effective in countering the one-sided, highly selective coverage of protest gatherings on broadcast television. The government-controlled media portrayed the protestors as violent and irresponsible, but the opposition video tapes revealed considerable police and military brutality, to which the protestors were reacting.

CASSETTES ARE CHEAP

The electronic media are evolving very rapidly, and we can create many opportunities to exploit these developments to disseminate visual and aural PR messages. Cassettes are remarkably cheap, easy to duplicate, and have a perceived value and substance that makes them difficult to throw into the circular file, the repository for so many written releases and junk mail.

Most cars and trucks are now equipped with cassette players, and it amazes me that more use is not made of this medium to publicize messages to commuters and others who spend long periods of captive time in their vehicles.

I have seen—rather, heard—audio cassettes used very effectively on the media test drives that are a feature of most new vehicle launches. You get an authoritative spokesman—perhaps the CEO or a senior engineer—to introduce and give background on the vehicle's features, which have considerably more impact because the media representative experiences them while using the product.

You can use similar techniques to reach specific key target audiences. Analysts and investment advisors are obvious prospects for audio tapes. They get flooded with written material—how much more effective to send them an entertaining tape linked to a topical peg, such as the publication of the annual report, in which the CEO talks in an informal, conversational tone about the company's achievements and prospects.

The target must be very strong-willed to resist playing such a tape and will probably do so in the car going to or from work, when you will have his or her almost undivided attention. There is also a sense of intimacy—of one-to-one communication—that enhances the impact of recorded audio messages.

Local Media Can Be Vital
Many small circulations add up to a lot of impact

In ploughing through hundreds of case histories to compile this book, it has saddened me to see how many PR people pride themselves on a mention in a major publication like *Time* or on one of the network talk shows and do not give the appropriate importance to publicity through the smaller local media.

These can, in combination, be very powerful, because they are read intensively and trusted. They become particularly important, even for big companies, when they circulate in an area of major operations, such as a plant location, because your employees will be among their readers.

If I have a client in this situation, I try to ensure priority delivery of everything we disseminate in the way of media releases—and copies of relevant internal company publications—to as many local journalists, by name, as possible. Even if their circulations are meagre compared to those of the big media guns, PR staff should still go out of their way to cultivate these local contacts and make them feel like the VIPs they really can be.

This is particularly important if labor relations are involved. Journalists instinctively side with employees against a corporation, even when they are doing their best to remain impartial. It's the natural order of things.

All those who form and communicate local opinion and can influence your workforce should identify on a personal level with the spokespeople for the corporation. If you get into a real crunch situation, the quality of your ongoing PR efforts toward your local media will pay off by getting you at least balanced coverage of what could be a nasty defensive PR situation, such as a strike, some corporate action that has impact on the environment, or any of the many other things that can bring an organization into conflict with its local community.

ENORMOUS OPPORTUNITIES

The opportunities for community PR are enormous, and some companies are very good at it. Others are very bad, because they chase the national headlines and forget about the vital people on their doorsteps.

Even an organization that is not doing a good job corporately in community PR will probably have significant numbers of employees doing their bit individually. The organization gains immensely by both recognizing and identifying itself with these individual efforts.

The Delaware Valley chemical company Rohm and Haas is a good example, with its appropriately named "People Practicing Good Chemistry" campaign, which focuses on employees' good works. It reflects an enlightened corporate philosophy that good business means not only rising sales and profits, but also building a foundation of goodwill and a sense of trust from the local level up.

This most praiseworthy PR campaign began internally, aimed first at the employees themselves. Employees volunteered to appear in a monthly video program and the workforce received a background kit on the program to supplement information disseminated through internal publications. Externally, the company launched a major advertising program in its area, with commercials featuring employees serving their communities in a variety of ways. The paid advertising was complimented by a full PR program of press releases, direct mail, videos, media tours, feature stories, receptions, and other media events.

PR THAT TRAVELS WELL

Companies that are considering similar ventures and that have a number of branches, plants, or other scattered facilities should consider following the Rohm and Haas example. The program should be structured right from the beginning to "travel well" and to be implemented easily away from head office at locations with probably fewer, less-experienced PR staff on the spot.

Catering to the needs of local media and taking advantage of the opportunities they offer can take many forms. It can be the way to get a regular column started, a particularly valuable medium for professionals such as lawyers, physicians in group medical practices, and investment advisers.

Zero in on a topic of general reader appeal that also reflects your specialist expertise, and generate several examples of how you would cover it in a weekly or monthly editorial column. Offer these to local editors, accompanying your samples with comprehensive details explaining why you would be an expert and reliable contributor.

Also offer to answer readers' letters. Indeed, you could use a question-and-answer format for the whole column—it works well for Ann Landers and can for you, too.

If you get an editor interested, you must play by editorial rules to keep this valuable PR medium working for you. That means never missing a deadline and, if you are going to be away on holiday or business, having reserve columns ready to maintain continuity through your absences. Do not offer your column to a competing publication in the same circulation area. Be impartial and accurate and do not plug yourself or your company. The exposure alone will work for you, if your name and company title, if appropriate, are featured.

IDENTIFY THE RIGHT CONTACTS

Local organizations—especially those that operate on a nonprofit basis—can get valuable long-term publicity if they just play the game right. That means identifying the publications and broadcasting media that will use material from you, the right people to whom you should send it, and the manner in which it should be prepared.

An event you wish to publicize can receive coverage in the bulletin-board sections on upcoming events or in the news and feature columns, with advance stories and pictures, coverage of the actual event, and then a follow-up on the results. Space and pace your local PR to maximize returns and emphasize the local angles.

Comparatively few head office PR operations take full advantage of local media opportunities, although the excuse of the large amount of work involved is no longer as valid with the aid that computers can give to customizing a standard release to the needs of different local media. You can, for example, draft a release about an event and program the software to insert in appropriate places the names of those attending and their home addresses. In this way, you can turn out customized releases for a number of local newspapers.

For example, if your organization has a national sales meeting, special training sessions, or other suitable activities bringing in people from different localities for something with a news angle, it is no great hassle to prepare one release and then customize it on a word processor for local media with the names, titles, and addresses of those attending. A good mail-merge program will do much of the work for you.

ZERO IN ON INDIVIDUALS

Awards for performance, publicized through local media by means of a release coupled with a picture, can generate a lot of coverage. I attended a big company's national awards ceremony for outstanding performances by dealer-service department managers. There was nothing in it to justify coverage in major publications, but customized local releases and pictures would have had strong appeal for a total of 65 newspapers in the home areas of the winners. That's too good a PR market to be passed by, although it usually is.

Local media can be very cost-effective as the *Denver Post* found out when it organized the "Ride the Rockies" bicycle tour as part of an aggressive marketing campaign in its circulation area. The broadcast coverage achieved—and that in the newspaper's competing medium—would have cost more than $20,000 in advertising time. It is accepted that editorial coverage is worth between three and five times as much as paid advertising because of its greater authority and the attention given to it by readers or listeners, so the true value just from broadcasting could have been nearly $100,000.

That program was really cost-effective, because the *Post* had to chip in only $61,200, with the other costs covered by registration fees from the riders who participated and from increased sales. Now that's the way to do it!

BUILDING A BETTER ZOO

Another admirable local effort was a campaign by Seattle's Woodland Park Zoo to generate public support for a bond issue to upgrade its facilities. It is also another example of how quality listening at the very beginning focuses a program effectively. Over the previous 15 years, voters had twice rejected capital construction bonds for the zoo. Research showed that they valued it most as an educational resource for children in the community, not for its ability to generate tourism and jobs, as might have been expected. When the campaign highlighted the educational aspect, the bond issue passed with a 67 percent approval rate and the PR generated substantial donations.

There was an imaginative multimedia mix of a brochure, posters, bumper stickers, information kits, paid radio spots, a slide show that was seen by 30 different community groups, and a widely distributed fact sheet. The organizers also gave many of us an important lesson in an information dissemination resource that we often overlook. Information kits were sent to the 100 largest employers in the area, so that they could carry the zoo's message in their employee-communication media.

POSTERS STOLEN

The posters were designed so that they could be attached to the yard signs of election candidates and proved so attractive that they were "stolen" by collectors, which generated extensive media coverage and significantly raised awareness and approval of the zoo bonds among voters just before the poll.

That was a great PR effort. The people of Seattle can thank PR for having as a community resource one of the best zoos in the world.

If your local PR project is good for the community, you can use what otherwise might be a prohibitively expensive medium—direct mail. Both political parties involved in the Seattle poll allowed 250,000 of the zoo's brochures to be included in their mailings.

Some organizations regularly distribute their promotional material with the monthly account statements mailed out by local banks, public utilities, and commercial companies. If it will not add to the postage cost and will fit in their envelopes, many organizations will be happy to cooperate in this way, and they will get the PR benefit of being identified with a good cause.

Section 6

Even a Mickey Mouse Watch-Wearing Communicator from Brooklyn Can Become a Publicist for Seven U.S. Presidents

Imaginative bank promotion program

A great PR opportunity comes around every four years in the United States, yet very few communicators take advantage of all the media attention and charisma that surrounds it. A classic exception was the campaign for new accounts staged by Citizens Savings & Loan in Akron that featured seven Ohio-born U.S. presidents.

The program was the brainchild of Chuck Olsen, a self-styled "Mickey Mouse watch-wearing communicator from Brooklyn", when he was director of communications at Investors Funding Corporation of New York, the parent of Citizens Savings.

The *Mid-Continent Banker* dubbed Chuck "a young man of vision from whose nimble brain spring imaginative promotional ideas", a description that includes the most desirable characteristics in any aspirant PR practitioner.

Chuck went on to become executive secretary of the Automotive Public Relations Council of the Motor and Equipment Manufacturers Association and it is no fault of his that much automotive PR has hit a trough of boring incompetence and lack of creativity. Indeed, when he heard that I was going to make such a scathing comment in this book, he turned the criticism into a PR opportunity and invited me to be the keynote speaker at his annual conference, drumming up attendance by telling his members that they would have the opportunity to counterattack.

THE LOCAL LINK

Chuck leaped onto the 1972 presidential-election bandwagon by proposing seven high-profile candidates of his own—all from Ohio—who had occupied the Oval Office. While Nixon and Mc-Govern were slugging it out on the campaign trail, existing and potential customers poured into Citizens Savings branches to cast their votes for the famous seven—Rutherford B. Hayes, James A. Garfield, Benjamin Harrison, William McKinley, Ulysses S. Grant, William Howard Taft, and Warren G. Harding.

Apart from the fun element of the mock election, Chuck's campaign focused strongly on Ohio pride, reminding locals that their state had made a substantial contribution to the presidential roster of history. The campaign forged a link between parochial patriotism and a local banking institution.

The come-on was that everyone who went into a Citizens Savings office to cast a vote also stood a chance of winning a free family trip to Washington, D.C. Note that the prize was a holiday for the whole family in a familiar American city. Research has shown that prizes of holidays for one or two people to far-away, exotic places are not as attractive as lower-cost, nearby holidays for entire families.

There appears to be built-in apprehension about winning a prize that brings with it potential problems and challenges, like being forced to select a partner to go on an overseas journey to potentially threatening destinations—still, for the majority of the population, a daunting prospect.

NON-THREATENING PRIZES

Often those of us who plan promotions are of a much more adventurous nature than are most people in our target markets. We forget that the majority of American people have yet to take a flight, and most have never been outside the United States.

The prize for Chuck's election promotion was one to which his target audience could aspire easily. It was also very affordable for the sponsoring bank, although it is now fairly easy to get cosponsors in the travel business to put up attractive trips as prizes if they think they will get adequate publicity returns.

The bank's consolation prizes were equally relevant and even more economical—American flags. That's another pointer from this case history—unless competition prizes are particularly lavish, pick trips or products that have a value that cannot easily be quantified. The flag consolation prizes cost Citizens Savings less than $50 in total, but no one accused the bank of being stingy. You just don't put a monetary value on the flag—or, incidentally, on a medal or a

Chuck Olsen's mock presidential election to promote the Citizens Savings & Loan Company in Akron, Ohio, was a good example of a local-level campaign with lots of activities that generated picture opportunities—for both press photographers and television crews.

certificate. They can be crafty, cost-saving—yet prestigious—prizes for many promotions.

"The whole scheme was an attention-grabber," recalls Chuck. "Once we got people into our branches to vote, then we could sell them on the bank's services."

LAUNCH PRESS CONFERENCE

He launched the program with a press conference at which actors resembling each of the seven presidents made election speeches and answered questions. Those one-minute campaign speeches were played on local radio stations with an equal time formula of 55 spots per candidate. Some of the spots were a lot more entertaining and attention-getting than was the rhetoric of Nixon and McGovern in the parallel real election.

If you use a hotel for a function, get the most out of its PR support facilities, which include the sign at the entrance (which Chuck uses here for his bank promotion), public address announcements, special catering, audiovisual equipment, internal television networks that show your videos in guest rooms, and so on. Be aggressive and imaginative to make the hotel staff enthusiastic and to motivate them to work with you. Get the bartender to concoct special commemorative cocktails with your corporate or product name, have unique labels printed to go on bottles of the house wine, customize the menu with corporate- or product-related dishes—the possibilities go on and on, if you explore them properly.

Carry the theme of a promotion to the outlets where the customers can translate the interest you have sparked into actual buying decisions for your client. Here Chuck had the election fever carried to his bank premises.

Professional actors were hired to play the roles of Ohio-born U.S. presidents throughout the mock election. If you hang a promotion on a charity peg, you often can get very good amateur actors to participate at little or no cost.

Each candidate also appeared ten times in newspaper advertisements, and there were other election propaganda paraphernalia,
including bumper stickers (such as "My Heart Belongs to Harding")
and campaign buttons. (Buttons are so cheap and effective that I'm
surprised more publicity people do not have their own machine to
produce them in-house.)

Make your giveaways collectible. Chuck's mock election campaign buttons were in such strong demand that they soon had to be
rationed to one per voter—thereby, of course, increasing interest in
them still further.

The promotion never lost sight of its prime objective of pulling
new customers into Citizens Savings offices, which were appropriately decorated like convention halls in red, white, and blue bunting,
with staff wearing similarly colored skimmers.

Chuck wisely extended the promotion's reach by staging debates
between the candidates in other venues to which he could be sure of
pulling large audiences, including shopping malls, Elks clubs, college
campuses, fraternity houses, and so on. The debates proved to be
such crowd pullers that the promotional fake election events had to
be timed so as not to clash with genuine political meetings (which
would have antagonized Nixon and McGovern campaigners).

THE EFFECTIVE FOLLOWUP

Another golden rule when doing any kind of promotion is to milk
it for exploitable followup data, and the Citizens Savings mock
election was a natural for that. When voters marked their ballot
slips to enter for the free holiday prize, they inevitably filled in
their names, addresses and telephone numbers, generating a useful
mailing list of potential customers.

Chuck's promotion soon started making news in its own right,
achieving editorial coverage in the print, radio, and television media.
Like any election campaign, he had a running news story to milk
for additional coverage by disseminating periodic releases on how
the candidates were doing. (Taft and Grant took an early lead in the
polls and Taft eventually won the election.)

Being a bank, Citizens Savings crunched the numbers to quantify
the results of the promotion, something other organizations often fail

to do. While it was running, the campaign helped to pull in nearly 1,500 new accounts and over $10 million in new money deposits. All for a $15,000 budget! How's that for cost-efficiency?

"This marketing communications program did not have a Goliath-sized budget, but it did produce impact worthy of David," says Chuck. "It was primarily a public relations vehicle, but integrated PR with advertising and sales promotion to give the marketing campaign maximum reach and impact.

"Above all, it was a fun campaign for everybody involved and a career high point for me, a Mickey Mouse watch-wearing communicator from Brooklyn who became publicist for seven U.S. Presidents!"

Look for the Hook
Design the news angle in from the start

Even the most imaginative and visually dramatic promotional stunts work much better if they are hung on a news peg. Your promotion then can move from being an artificial public relations exercise and can become a real-life event of sufficient interest or substance to merit editorial coverage in its own right, without the need for hype.

That can happen by accident. It is much better, though, if the news angle is designed in from the beginning or provides the nucleus around which the creative promotion is constructed.

If the model Starship Enterprise I had built for a sponsor had decapitated the marketing director, as it threatened to do when it went out of control, my *Star Trek* stunt would have become internationally newsworthy, although the client reaction would not have been favorable! Far more fruitful was when the 10-foot-tall stuffed gorilla I used to promote the *King Kong* movie remake got catapulted onto front pages when it was stolen.

The ape had been only modestly successful as a display item at the premiere and in theater foyers. My attempts to get celebrities photographed with it had failed to generate much media coverage. However, when the creature was stolen one night, the publicity bandwagon really started rolling.

Members of a sports club stole it from the theater, then their rivals stole it from them—and then it disappeared altogether. I got excellent media coverage for both thefts and kept the pot boiling by offering a substantial reward. When my promotions manager and the local media had milked the story far more than it really was worth, the ape rematerialized one night back at the cinema. I suspect my promotions man had orchestrated much of the action, but it was all such good fun that nobody—including the reporters—probed too deeply.

INFLATABLE KING KONG

Jack Mayo of San Diego has a far better King Kong story hung on a really great news peg. Jack is professor of Marketing Public Relations at National University, a successful author, and a former chair of the Public Relations Society of America's Professional Development Forum, has degrees from four universities and taught at five, and in general has a resume that sparkles with academic and professional achievements. Yet, he still is best known for his King Kong stunt with New York's Empire State Building, another example of how creative PR can outpull almost anything else in memorability.

"King Kong was a serious business," Jack keeps on protesting. "It's OK for people to think that it was just a crazy stunt, but it only worked because it was a very serious project, well planned and executed carefully."

This case history explains why only two percent of all the new products certified at the U.S. Patent Office every year become commercially successful. However brilliantly innovative the other 98 percent may be, they won't go anywhere without good marketing, of which PR can be a vital element.

Jack's client, Robert Keith Vicino, realized that, even if you build the best mousetrap, the world will not beat a path to your door unless you market it properly. That's why the San Diego entrepreneur used PR so effectively.

Robert Vicino invented cold-air inflatable advertising displays and turned the idea into a profitable small business through the Pepsi Challenge. He made the 20-foot Pepsi cans and 30-foot bottles used in that mammoth promotion. They were so successful that soon America was swarming with imitators making inflatable cans and bottles and committing business suicide by undercutting each other's prices.

PASSIVE PROPS DON'T GET EFFECTIVE PUBLICITY

Robert went back to the drawing board and came up with the concept of "air sculpture"—customized inflatables in all shapes and sizes. The entrepreneur publicized his new product line with what appeared to be a brilliant promotional stunt—he built a giant replica of the entertainment industry's premier trophy, the Oscar, and displayed it on top of the Dorothy Chandler pavilion in Los Angeles during the Academy Awards ceremony, one of the world's most-publicized annual events.

Robert Vicino's inflatable got a lot of attention from the crowds, and it featured prominently on network television—but it did very little for his business. It was dominated by its news peg and became just a passive prop, unable to compete with all the glitz and glamour of Hollywood's big night.

When Jack Mayo was retained, he began the marketing/PR consultancy task with the boring-but-essential, fact-finding legwork that is required before the fun part begins and the creative juices can be allowed to flow in the right direction.

"You must always start by examining a client's competitive position," Jack emphasizes. "Measuring Robert's strengths and weaknesses alongside those of his competition produced the essential information for our marketing strategy."

Robert was convinced that he and his competitors would eventually go bankrupt if they fought to produce ever-lower-priced replicas of cans and bottles. Fortunately, his ability to make custom inflatable shapes could virtually guarantee his survival, because it was unlikely that his competitors could find a way around his patented manufacturing technique.

"It's pure business logic to maximize the sales of a product that cannot be copied and our task was to develop a marketing strategy to create both an *awareness* of Robert's new product and develop that into a *demand* for it," Jack recalls.

"Our marketing research showed that the potential buyers who would most benefit from custom-shaped giant product replicas were corporations owned by the consumer products conglomerates. They nearly all employed Madison Avenue mass marketing agencies."

GO TO THE SOURCE

"So if you see a massive Ronald McDonald on top of a fast food stand in San Francisco, a giant tire at a tire dealership in Detroit or a 10-foot tall Spuds McKenzie over a liquor store in Alaska, those point-of-purchase advertising displays are usually ordered from Madison Avenue.

"None of Robert's potential customers attended the Academy Awards in Hollywood, but if his product demonstration could be repeated in New York we could achieve our objectives."

An inflatable replica of the Statue of Liberty was considered, but rejected in favor of a King Kong, because there was a strong news peg available. Radio City Music Hall was commemorating the golden anniversary of its premiere of the movie classic, so it was natural to jump on that bandwagon and recreate Kong's celebrated climb up the Empire State building.

Jack Mayo followed another golden rule of PR promotions—if you've got a great idea, shop around for other sponsors who also might like it, so that your client gets the benefits without picking up the whole tab. The Empire State had office vacancies on almost every floor at the time, so owner Harry Helmsley was glad to help finance the stunt in return for the exposure it would give his building. Transport costs were another trade-off, with World Airways Freight moving the inflatable ape and the staff accompanying it from the west to the east coasts in return for Kong's subsequent appearance at their corporate headquarters in Oakland.

CELEBRITY ENDORSEMENT

Almost any stunt gains credibility when endorsed by civic leaders or other celebrities, so New York mayor Ed Koch's blessing was sought, along with that of the National Landmarks Commission. It is always a good rule to get such endorsements, and they are usually easier to obtain if you make a donation to charity—and as long as your promotion is not dangerous, in poor taste, or just plain silly.

Even for promotions far less complicated than the King Kong one, you must have a detailed public relations plan so that there is a structure and timetable that ensures that everyone knows what has to be done—and who is responsible for doing it.

Jack Mayo's plan was very detailed, listing corporate objectives, the various target publics, and so on. Over 200 prospective clients for inflatable product replicas were identified and invited to attend—not just to see Kong swinging from the Empire State, of course, but to bring them into contact with Vicino's organization and to develop sales leads in a very positive atmosphere.

These prime targets were entertained at a party they will always remember on the 86th floor observation deck—physically and emotionally elevating them into privileged VIP status.

EXPOSURE WORTH MILLIONS

A separate media plan was created, exploiting the pre-event picture opportunities as well as those on the big day itself. A comprehensive press kit was prepared, with lots of background on the company and its unique line of customized inflatables. The media coverage was worth millions of dollars, with global exposure on television, the wire services, and in newspapers and magazines around the world. The story made both the *Good Morning America* and the *Today* shows.

Of course, after all this build-up you are expecting me to report that everything went smoothly as the 22,750 square feet of inflatable, vinyl-coated nylon were hauled into position atop the Empire State, the air was blown in and Kong's yard-long teeth flashed a smile down on Madison Avenue, where buyers stampeded to place orders.

Well, it wasn't quite like that.

The riggers, dangling a quarter mile above the Manhatten pavements, had to battle with high winds. A restraining wire got tangled around Kong's left leg, puncturing the fabric minutes before a packed press conference attended by 125 reporters and 35 television crews.

Then it rained, adding to the technical problems and washing out several further attempts. Kong was not permanently inflated until six days later, and the firm's home-town paper in San Diego wrote it all off as an embarrassing fiasco.

Meanwhile, back in New York.

EXPLOITING DISASTER

The stunt was such an imaginative, fun event that the screw-ups didn't really matter to the prime target market. Anyway, Jack Mayo's team turned potential disaster into a strong running news story.

The Madison Avenue marketing firms knew that they would not be putting such elaborate inflatables on top of wind-whipped skyscrapers. Thanks to the promotion, they were made *aware* of the new product and soon created their own *demand* for it. Those were the true objectives; suspending the ape from the Empire State was but a means of achieving them.

On the sixth day of the promotion, Kong rose to the top of the Empire State Building and was "parked" there until the crowd flow eased. Then Jack Mayo gave the project another publicity kick by moving Kong to Central Park, so that people could be photographed in front of him.

That provides another lesson. If you have a highly visual prop, literally and figuratively bring it down to ground level and offer the public the opportunity for happy snaps. Every picture taken could expose your message to a score or more people and generate strong word of mouth over an extended period.

Vicino's company was inundated with orders and had to move to bigger premises as it spearheaded a whole new mini-industry of giant inflatable product replicas.

The vacancies in the Empire State Building were filled within 30 days.

Kong went on to be a star attraction, earning fat rental fees and making the promotion not only self-liquidating, but also highly profitable.

This was believed at the time to be the only promotional stunt to make the front page of *the New York Times*, and there is an enormously long list of other print and broadcast media exposure it got around the world.

SPECIFIC OBJECTIVES

The real point is that this was not just a media space grabber but a properly organized, professional PR promotion that achieved specific objectives by alerting its prime target market to a new product, establishing a demand to generate profitable business for the client.

As Jack Mayo still drums into his students; "You must have a marketing method for PR to be effective".

INHIBITING CONSERVATISM

This tremendous publicity stunt was so successful that Jack Mayo was inspired to go on to even bigger and better things—but encountered the conservatism that so often inhibits imaginative PR of all kinds.

He wanted to dress up the famous TransAmerica building in San Francisco with inflatable shapes to turn it into the world's biggest Christmas Tree. Nearly a year of planning went into the project, with all the logistics worked out. Timed for the Christmas season, the promotion could have been highly cost-effective in generating editorial exposure to increase public awareness of the client and boosting its community relations.

It was decided instead to spend more money on an advertising spread in *Time* magazine. Although the ad was great, they paid more to go the conventional and predictably safe advertising route rather than speculate on a great idea that could achieve potentially more high-impact and cost-effective editorial exposure.

There is another lesson here. Senior management, who will ultimately make decisions about any kind of promotion, need to be involved early and motivated to give their support—with firm commitments before there is a substantial investment in both time and money.

The circumstances surrounding the proposed giant San Francisco Christmas Tree were beyond Jack Mayo's control, but, as a general rule, build into any ambitious program an internal PR effort to sell the concept initially to either your own or your client's management as the case may be. Turn them on and then get them firmly committed so that they are with you all the way.

Influencing Investors
How to shift stock prices and preserve confidence

If clever PR people keep on demonstrating how effectively they can influence investor attitudes toward a company, the profession at last might start participating as fully in boardroom decision-making as it deserves to do.

There are now too many examples of PR successes in influencing investors for other disciplines to ignore the power of enlightened corporate communications. Particularly important in recent years have been the achievements in making investors, brokers, and analysts understand the underlying reasons why companies experience crises, so that more attention is paid to longer-term potential and less to short-term stock movements and trading figures.

The tyranny of the quarterly report for too long has bedevilled American business strategy and allowed overseas competitors, notably the Japanese, to be more venturesome and far-sighted. If American business is to meet the global challenges of the next decade, then the power of good PR to disseminate information on which valid investment decisions can be made must play a larger role.

The evidence is convincing. A Texas pharmaceutical company used a multimedia mix of fact cards, slide presentations, face-to-face meetings, media releases, and direct mail to build confidence during a temporary downturn in its fortunes. As a direct consequence, brokers and analysts made recommendations to buy, and the stock price was kept at the levels justified by a proper understanding of the facts rather than emotional reaction to temporary difficulties.

OVERCOMING NEGATIVE ATTITUDES

A high-tech company saw its stock plunge after losing a major contract but adopted an enlightened PR strategy that transformed the negative press comments on its prospects and the investor perception that the management team was unstable and its technology becoming stale.

Proven PR techniques—including internationally shown slide presentations and radically different annual and quarterly reports containing far more information than is legally required—helped the company to outperform its industry-average price-to-earnings ratio and show remarkable increases in its stock value during a year of flat earnings.

A major corporation in the metals and chemicals business fought off a hostile takeover bid and got both shareholders and employees solidly behind management by means of a broad PR program that communicated all major developments very rapidly to the prime target audiences.

The strategy included creating a War Room to give a sense of urgency and vitality to the communication function. A paramount consideration was that employees hear all the important information about their company before it hit the media. Over 100 employee volunteers participated in a telephone campaign to brief shareholders, and there was a major effort to make top management available to the media for interviews and to give journalists frank and comprehensive background briefings.

Charts were used to demonstrate graphically how the company was progressing on the road back to profitability and being fully competitive again.

THE PERSONAL TOUCH PAYS OFF

A computer company that was still struggling after having emerged from bankruptcy filing moved fast and efficiently to disseminate news about its losses and the reasons for them. Instead of relying solely on media coverage, the company telephoned and hand-distributed news releases of all major corporate developments directly to key people in the investment community.

This competently executed PR strategy maintained investor confidence through a succession of crises until the company could start to produce the figures that demonstrated its potential for growth.

EMPLOYEE SUPPORT ESSENTIAL

The main lesson to be learned from these and similar experiences is that mobilizing the support of employees is essential for such corporate PR efforts to be successful, even if the main target is seen to be the external investment community.

Speed and frankness also are vital if a company is to take the initiative—and keep it—in the dissemination of information about its performance. This principle applies even more in bad and traumatic times than it does when things are going well. A secretive management style that is evasive in dealing with the media and the investment community results in damaging rumor, speculation and loss of confidence. It takes courage to rush out with your own bad news, but when the news is properly explained and backgrounded, confidence can be retained under seemingly the most adverse of situations.

Promoting Deadly Habits
How the developing nations suffer from PR

Let's end by paying tribute to and learning lessons from the most consistently brilliant PR of probably any industry anywhere in the world. Against all odds and rational calculations, the tobacco industry's communicators have continued to promote with great success a product that has no material benefits for the user and that annually kills or seriously damages the quality of life of more Americans than have died in all the wars this country has fought. Their product causes a million premature deaths worldwide each year. They continue to aggravate America's most serious health problem, and only the promoters of alcoholic beverages come close to rivaling their success.

Now that their wings are being clipped by restrictions and legal action, the publicity focus is moving from the developed to the developing nations, where vast potential markets are being exploited by marketing and PR expertise.

No one uses research results to prove a case better than the tobacco industry to pursue its own interests. The challenge increases as medical proof of the health hazards of tobacco outweighs the industry's own sponsored research.

Celebrity endorsements, sports sponsorships, music and other cultural events, public opinion surveys, political lobbying, community projects, peer figures, the distribution of free samples, press releases—name a PR device, and the tobacco industry has used it to publicize its products and counter its critics.

It has taken the opponents of smoking inordinately long to realize one of the prime principles of PR—that it is very difficult to promote a negative message. Only comparatively recently has the emphasis switched in a number of effective campaigns from promulgating the dangers of smoking to publicizing the positive benefits to be gained from quitting.

INDEX

Here's how to receive your free catalog and save money on your next book order from Scott, Foresman and Company.

Simply mail in the response card below to receive your free copy of our latest catalog featuring computer and business books. After you've looked through the catalog and you're ready to place your order, attach the coupon below to receive $1.00 off the catalog price of Scott, Foresman and Company Professional Publishing Group computer and business books.

□   YES, please send me my *free* catalog of your latest computer and business books!

Name (please print) _____

Company _____

Address _____

City _____ State _____ Zip _____

Mail response card to: Scott, Foresman and Company
　　　　　　　　　　　 Professional Books Group
　　　　　　　　　　　 1900 East Lake Avenue
　　　　　　　　　　　 Glenview, IL 60025

PUBLISHER'S COUPON　　　　　NO EXPIRATION DATE

SAVE $1.00

Limit one per order. Good only on Scott, Foresman and Company Professional Books Group publications. Consumer pays any sales tax. Coupon may not be assigned, transferred, or reproduced. Coupon will be redeemed by Scott, Foresman and Company Professional Publishing Group, 1900 East Lake Avenue, Glenview, IL 60025.

Customer's Signature _____